CLEVELAND LANDMARKS SERIES

VOLUME I

THE TERMINAL TOWER COMPLEX

BY JIM TOMAN & DAN COOK

Publishing Information

Printed in the United States of America

ISBN — 0-936760-01-X

Library of Congress Catalog Card Number 80-81212

Published by:

Cleveland Landmarks Press, Inc.
P.O. Box 9152
Cleveland, Ohio 44137

FIRST PRINTING

Acknowledgements

The authors wish to express their appreciation to the following who gave of their time, and without whose help and encouragement this work would not have come to print:

Gene Krantz and Dick Green of U.S. Realty Investments, Doug Tindal and Al Kalish of Ostendorf-Morris Company, Mark Nylander of the Stouffer Corporation, John O'Neill and Jerry Grdina of Ress Realty, John Wilson, Norm Noblet, and Marion Ratnoff of The Higbee Company, and Wilburt Murray, Bob Smurthwaite, and Nick Marchese of the United States Postal Service.

The authors are also indebted to Bob Love of The Cleveland **Press,** to Judy Chelnick of The Shaker Historical Museum, and to Bob Kanner of Kanner Industries for their valuable assistance.

A final and special word of thanks goes to Bruce Domski for his art work, to Jack Muslovski for his many hours of assistance with photographic work, to Brian Azzarello and Claire Thompson for valuable recommendations toward textual clarity, and in particular to Tom Luckay for rewrites and polishing.

Photographs used in this work have come from a variety of sources. Initials used after each photograph correspond to the following: The Cleveland Picture Collection of the Cleveland Public Library (CPL); Greater Cleveland Growth Association (GCGA); United States Postal Service Archives (USPS); Western Reserve Historical Society (WRHS); The Stouffer Corporation (SC); The Higbee Company (HC); Richard J. Cook Collection (RJC); Ken Kessler Collection (KK); Jack Muslovski (JM); the Shaker Historical Museum (SHM), and the authors (not marked).

Photographs on the inside of the front and rear covers are from the collection of the Greater Cleveland Growth Association.

PREFACE

Recent years have not been happy ones for the City of Cleveland. Unfortunate events such as the fire on the Cuyahoga River, or the mayor's accidentally setting his hair afire, have drawn unfavorable attention to the city by both the national media and the gag writers for the entertainment industry.

The political climate in the city, characterized for so many years by a spirit of confrontation, the stunning reality of the city's financial default, and the exodus of some important industrial headquarters, have all combined to deepen the gloom that pervades the local scene.

It has often been stated that one of Cleveland's most severe faults is the fact that its citizens over-react to the city's problems and ignore its strengths. Clevelanders seem to suffer from a type of urban insecurity. They know their city has problems, they hear them repeated in the press, and they come to believe that the city's future is bleak.

This image tends to have a far greater impact than it deserves. It seems to pervade not just the ordinary citizens' outlook, but also to act as a damper on the energies and commitments of the city's political and business leadership. Conservatism has been the hallmark of the city's life for the past fifty years.

This series, of which the present volume represents the first installment, is unashamedly dedicated to an "up with Cleveland" theme. Cleveland surely has its share of problems, but within it are assets and resources that are more than sufficient to once again bring the community to the pinnacle of greatness.

Cleveland Landmarks Press has but one purpose: to focus attention on positive attributes of the city. In so doing it may contribute to the restoration of faith in the city's future and prompt renewed and broader commitment to that goal.

This series will not satisfy those who are seeking a definitive work based on scholarly methods of historical research into primary sources. It is not intended to fill that need. Rather, its goal is to tell its story in popular fashion. Hopefully, in doing so, there has been no sacrifice of accuracy.

The Terminal Tower Complex was selected for the topic of the first volume because it is Cleveland's most familiar landmark. Future volumes will treat other city landmarks, those of steel and mortar, and those which attest to the city's commitment to all those things that contribute to a fuller life. Together, these help make the city the truly great place it is.

To all those who genuinely care about the city, we recommend that they take to heart the words of Daniel H. Burnham, the architect who helped develop the city's civic center in the early years of this century:

> *Make no little plans; they have no magic to stir men's blood and probably themselves will not be realized. Make big plans; aim high in hope and work, remembering that a noble, logical plan once recorded will never die, but long after we are gone will be a living thing asserting itself with growing insistence.*

May all Clevelanders once again "make big plans."

In the early years of the century, the southwest quadrant of Public Square was ringed with a collection of aging and unimpressive buildings. (CPL)

The look of Public Square had altered dramatically by 1930. Here Hotel Cleveland and the soaring Terminal Tower await the construction of The Higbee Company store to balance the architecture of the new look at the city's center. (CPL)

CHAPTER I

The Face of the City is Changed

A visitor to Cleveland during World War I, as he travelled down Euclid Avenue, undoubtedly would have been impressed by the stately homes that lined the city's main thoroughfare.

But when he arrived at Public Square, the heart of the city, he would have found little there to increase his appreciation for Cleveland. As he looked across the Square from its northeast corner he would have seen only a collection of aged buildings, grime-coated with years' accumulation of smoke and soot, and disfigured by ugly billboards proclaiming their tenants' wares.

If the same visitor were to have returned in 1931, his view and his viewpoint both would have been changed. Then he would have seen the soaring Terminal Tower Building, flanked on the west by the Hotel Cleveland and on the east by The Higbee Company department store. The city had shed its big town look, and had now clearly taken on the appearance of a major American metropolis.

Ever since that day of June 28, 1930 when the Terminal Complex was formally dedicated, Clevelanders have been proud to acknowledge the Terminal Tower as **the** symbol of the city. Rightly have they chosen, for the Terminal Complex represented at the time of its construction the most ambitious and extensive integrated building complex in the nation; the famous Rockefeller Center in New York City would not come onto the scene for several more years. Not only was Cleveland's most famous landmark monumental in its size, but it also typified the reality of the city at that time: a pacesetter in American life.

But it almost did not happen.

The Mall, as viewed from Terminal Tower's upper floors, is a tree-lined, fountain-filled expanse of green in the midst of a bustling downtown. (JM)

Today not too many Clevelanders are familiar with the term "Group Plan." It stands for the development of civic and governmental buildings that stretch northward from Lakeside Avenue between East Sixth and Ontario Streets. But during the first quarter of the century, the Group Plan was a major focus of the city's newspapers and of the public's attention.

The brainchild of one of Cleveland's greatest mayors, Tom L. Johnson (1901-1909), the Group Plan, under the guiding influence of noted architects Daniel H. Burnham and Frederick L. Olmsted, provided for the clearing of 101 acres of land occupied by a collection of aging private homes and commercial buildings. In their place would rise a grouping of civic buildings united in architectural idiom. These were to be connected by a large open expanse of green, known as The Mall.

The first of the Group Plan buildings to be completed was the Federal Building, opened in 1908 at the corner of Superior Avenue and Public Square. Other buildings in the plan include: Cleveland City Hall and the Cuyahoga County Court House on Lakeside Avenue, the Public Auditorium and Cleveland Board of Education Building along East Sixth Street, and the main Cleveland Public Library Building on Superior Avenue.

Another building had been proposed as part of the Group Plan, a railroad station. It would have been located at the northern end of The Mall between the Court House and the City Hall buildings. The outbreak of World War I had delayed its start, but in 1916 voters gave the project the go-ahead.

Onto the scene at that time came the Van Sweringen brothers (more about them in the next chapter) with a proposal of their own for a railroad passenger facility. It was to be built at the southwest quadrant of Public Square.

The two proposals were in conflict, and the city took up sides. The dispute, which became quite bitter at times, was finally settled by the voters on January 10, 1919. They approved the "Ordinance of 1919," agreeing with the Public Square site, by a vote of 30,758 to 19,916.

The ordinance cleared the way for the Terminal Group project. It set forth a multitude of details about the site development, the construction process, and the eventual upkeep of the facility. As a result of the vote Clevelanders gained in two ways. They kept a clear vista of the lakefront from The Mall, and they gained their city's most famous landmark, the Terminal Tower.

Work on the Terminal project actually began in 1920, with about 1,400 buildings being razed from some 35 acres of land. Workers cleared the entire area west of Ontario Street extending downward to Canal Street at the edge of the Cuyahoga River. Several streets disappeared from the map, the best known of which were Champlain and Michigan Streets. Many familiar old buildings were reduced to rubble.

Westward from East 34th Street and Pittsburgh Avenue, retaining walls were built to provide for a clear railroad access to the new project site. A total of 22 bridges were erected. Altogether 17 miles of new railroad trackage was laid, from the Village of Collinwood on the east to the Village of Linndale on the west. New suburban stations for railroad passengers were erected in both Linndale and East Cleveland. A large new facility for handling foods and produce was constructed at East 37th Street, the Northern Ohio Food Terminal.

And right at the center, buildings began to rise.

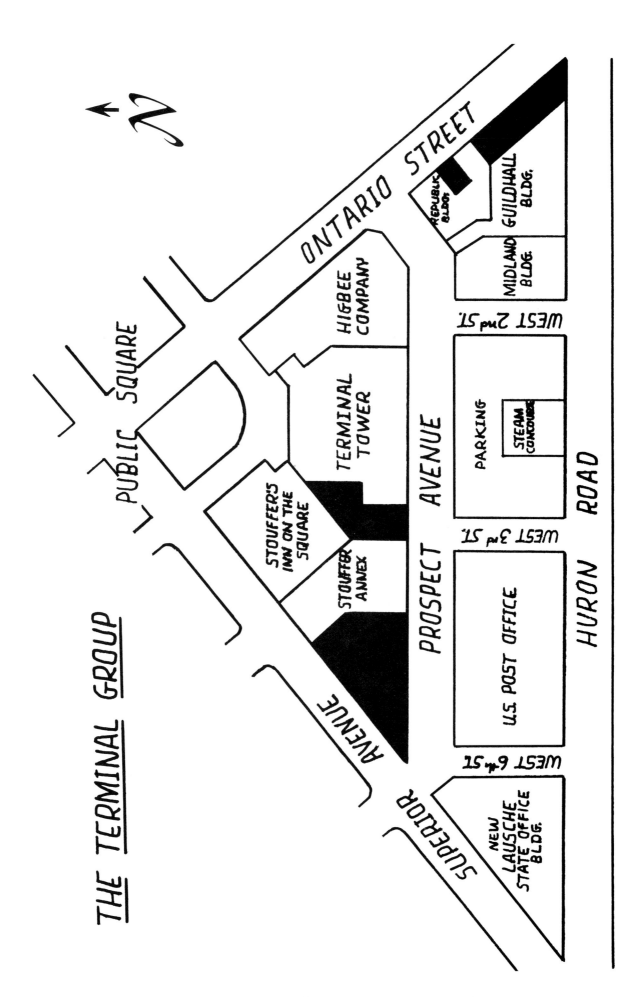

THE TERMINAL GROUP

N

PUBLIC SQUARE

ONTARIO STREET

HIGBEE COMPANY

TERMINAL TOWER

STOUFFER'S INN ON THE SQUARE

STOUFFER ANNEX

PROSPECT AVENUE

REPUBLIC BLDG.

GUILDHALL BLDG.

MIDLAND BLDG.

WEST 2nd ST.

PARKING

STEAM CONCOURSE

WEST 3rd ST.

U.S. POST OFFICE

HURON ROAD

SUPERIOR AVENUE

WEST 6th ST.

NEW LAUSCHE STATE OFFICE BLDG.

The Terminal Tower Complex transformed the features of the city, from the edges of Public Square right down to the banks of the Cuyahoga River. By the early 1940's the Tower had already become the unofficial symbol of the city. (CPL)

Today when one discusses the Terminal Group, he is referring to the entire downtown project, and not just its most famous member, the Terminal Tower. Also included is the cavernous Cleveland Union Terminal, Stouffer's Inn on the Square, The Higbee Company, the Republic, Guildhall and Midland Buildings, and the United States Post Office.

The perimeter of the development consists of Superior Avenue and Public Square on the north, Ontario Street on the East, Huron Road on the south, and West Sixth Street on the west. Two of these roadways, Prospect Avenue and Huron Road, are actually bridges built over the railroad tracks and the station facilities. To the south, beyond and below Huron Road, is the site of the former coach yards and of the ancillary train personnel facilities.

The entire Terminal Complex is vast, comprising a total of 3,375,000 square feet of useable space. Construction, which went on from 1920 until 1934 when the Post Office Building was completed, cost $179,000,000. If that cost were converted into 1980 dollars, the price tag would soar to a total of nearly $1,500,000,000 (1½

billion dollars).

Another insight into the size of the complex can be gained from the number of people who work within its boundaries. About 13,000 people spend each work day there; another 45,000 people daily pass through the buildings.

The Terminal Complex is clearly monumental in its physical dimensions. Yet it is also a monument in another way as well. It stands as a symbol of the kind of adventurous spirit that was a hallmark of the city of Cleveland during the first third of the Twentieth Century. That spirit is personified in a very special way by the two brothers who built the Terminal group.

When the complex was dedicated in 1930, a giant reception for civic leaders was held in the Union Terminal's main concourse. The guest list comprised Cleveland's Who's Who of the day. William Ganson Rose, noted civic leader and historian, was master of ceremonies.

Notable, however, for their absence from the celebration that day were the two men who made it all happen, the Van Sweringen brothers. The Terminal story is really their story as well.

CHAPTER 2

The Van Sweringen Brothers

The Van Sweringen story begins, not in the City of Cleveland, but about 50 miles to the southwest, in rural Wayne County, Ohio. There, on April 24, 1879, Orris Paxton Sweringen was born, the second son of James T. (prophetically, for "Tower") and Jennie Curtis Sweringen. Two years later a third son, Mantis James, was born. The two brothers were inseparable companions throughout their lives.

In addition to the two brothers, the Sweringen Family consisted of one older brother, Herbert, and two sisters, Edith and Carrie. The family moved north to Geneva, Ohio. It was there that Mrs. Sweringen died. Seeking a brighter future, James Sweringen packed up his five children and, in 1886, moved to Cleveland. They settled in a home on Willson Avenue (the street's name was later changed to East 55th Street) near Cedar Avenue.

Brothers Orris Paxton (always called O.P.) and Mantis James (called M.J.) attended first Bolton School and later Fairmount School. Money was in short supply for the family, so the brothers sought to supplement their income by delivering newspapers in the area of what is now Shaker Heights.

This early experience, in the lands abandoned by the members of the Shaker religious colony, was to have a lasting impression on the brothers. By 1889 the local Shaker group, in what was then known as North Union Village, had shrunk to less than 30 members, prompting them to disperse to other Shaker colonies in Ohio and New York after placing their land up for sale.

The Van Sweringen Brothers, Orris Paxton on the left and Mantis James on the right.   (CPL)

The property, totally 1,366 acres, was sold to a local real estate firm in 1889 for a grand total of $316,000. Little settlement took place on the land after the sale. As the brothers delivered their papers, they trudged through largely open land.

In 1894 the brothers left school and went to work for the Bradley Chemical Company. It was housed in Cleveland's tallest structure of the day, the Society for Savings Building, located on Public Square.

For some reason, although they did well at their jobs, O.P. and M.J. sought a more challenging kind of life. They turned their attention to real estate. Their first ventures were in nearby Lakewood, Ohio, but there they did not meet the success for which they had hoped. The properties with which they were involved ended up in foreclosure actions.

Though stung by the setback, the brothers decided to put past failure behind them and start anew. To herald this second try, they decided to change even their names, and it was at this time that the aristocratic "Van" (which had been dropped from the Sweringen birthright much earlier) was restored.

The second change they adopted was to shift their attention from the west side of the city to the eastern suburbs, where they developed North Park Boulevard in Cleveland Heights. This time they met with success. The next project was to be Fairmount Boulevard, but they realized that to make this development of fine homes a success they would have to secure public transportation; it was just too far out of town in those days to be an attractive residential site without convenient streetcar service.

O.P. and M.J. approached John J. Stanley, president of the Cleveland Railway Company, and persuaded him to build what became the Fairmount Boulevard streetcar line. With public transit assured, the Fairmount development became another triumph for the brothers. They were no longer poor men.

Fond memories of their boyhood days on the Shaker plateau drew them back to that area, making it their next target for development. In 1905 they took an option on the land, and in 1906 they bought the acreage for $1,000,000.

In the Shaker lands, the brothers had their chance to develop not just one boulevard, but to plan an entire community. They succeeded remarkably well at their task. Their planning was truly extraordinary, and Shaker Heights developed into one of the nation's first model examples of a planned suburban community.

The Van Sweringens designed a community of broad boulevards and gracefully curving streets, with large lots and land set aside for recreational purposes. They created a strict zoning code requiring that each residence built be of a design distinct from every other one. They specified that no home could be built for a cost less than $17,000 (an amount that today would be equivalent to about $140,000). These provisions remained in effect throughout the Vans' period of control. As a result Shaker Heights grew into a distinctive community, gracefully laid out, and marked by homes of architectural merit.

The transformation of Shaker Heights, Ohio from a wilderness into a model, planned community was due largely to the Van Sweringen brothers. Here is a view of Shaker Square in 1929. A few years earlier the Square had been a traffic circle nearly surrounded by open fields.   (SHM)

The development of Shaker Square was a further sign of the brothers' forward thinking, an archtype of the suburban shopping centers of today. They found a harmonious way to join residential and commercial properties. They provided shopping convenience while not infringing on the residential character they wished to maintain for their model community.

Shaker Heights did not sprout overnight. At first, lots in the development were selling rather slowly. O.P. and M.J. recognized that the persistent cause was a lack of convenient public transportation. They turned to John Stanley once again, but this time they were rebuffed. Stanley pointed out that running streetcars into sparsely populated areas was not the way to increase his company's profits. He told the brothers: get the people first; then the streetcar line would be built.

The Vans, however, had dreamt of their Shaker development for far too long to be stymied by this rejection. If the Cleveland Railway Company would not build a streetcar line for them, they would have to build one themselves.

Their study of the area had suggested to them that the natural ravine west of Shaker Square provided for a logical setting for a rail line. It could continue through Kingsbury Run and on to downtown Cleveland.

In order to get the tracks for their transit line into the downtown area, however, the brothers realized that they would have to get permission from the Nickel Plate Railroad to cross their existing right-of-way. They approached the railroad with their request, but were shocked at what they regarded as too high a price for their rather modest need.

At the time the Nickel Plate Railroad was a subsidiary line of the larger New York Central Railroad. The courts had ordered that the new York Central divest itself of its interest in the smaller line. This provided a natural opening for the enterprising brothers. They simply bought the Nickel Plate Railroad for $8,500,000.

The Van Sweringen holdings grew as their vistas broadened. They had started out in the real estate business. In order to make that effort a success, they were forced into the streetcar business, and to bring that venture to completion, they were nudged into the railroad business.

By 1916 the brothers found themselves the owners of a railroad property that stretched 513 miles from Buffalo, New York to Chicago, Illinois. All this had come about in order to gain access to a mere five miles of trackage rights for their streetcar line.

At the time they took over the Nickel Plate, it had been a marginally profitable line. They brought to it some astute management under the leadership of J. J. Bernet. The line was rebuilt and revitalized, rapidly becoming a highly profitable enterprise for the Vans. (Today the Nickel Plate is part of the Norfolk and Western Railroad — a line which continues to operate at a profit.)

With the right-of-way finally in their control, the Van Sweringens began construction of their streetcar line in 1916. Originally called the Cleveland Interurban Railroad Company (later renamed the Shaker Heights Rapid Transit and today the Shaker and Van Aken Lines of the Regional Transit Authority), the line began its operations on April 11, 1920.

The line's need for a downtown terminal, and the brothers' ongoing discussions with other railroad officials, prompted them to explore the feasibility of developing a major new railroad passenger station downtown. This would serve not just their own rapid transit lines but all of the railroads serving the city. Their attention focused on Public Square.

The Public Square site offered two advantages to the brothers which the proposed Group Plan railroad facility on the lakefront could not match. The lakefront station, on public land to be built at public expense, offered no profits to the real estate conscious brothers. Secondly, the lakefront location did not provide their lines with a convenient access because they entered the city from the southeast.

Thus was born the Van Sweringen proposal for the Public Square facility; as was mentioned in the previous chapter, it was approved by the voters in 1919.

When their Shaker Heights line began its operations in 1920, the Public Square terminal was just entering its construction phase. This made an alternate route into downtown a temporary necessity. At East 34th Street, its tracks left the valley floor and followed a ramp up to Pittsburgh Avenue where they joined those of the Cleveland Railway's Broadway Avenue streetcar line into downtown. That ramp, unused since 1930, can still be seen today as a remnant of the line's early routing.

All the while the Shaker Heights Village properties were being developed, the rapid transit line being built, and the station plans being laid, the Vans still found time to become further involved in the railroad industry. They took over the Chesapeake and Ohio Railroad (the C & O, today part of the Cleveland-based Chessie System), as well as the Erie, Pere Marquette and the Wheeling and Lake Erie Railroads. In 1930, they purchased their last railroad property, the Missouri Pacific. Altogether their railroad empire had grown to include 27,000 miles of trackage. They even took over control of the city's transit system, the Cleveland Railway Company. When the Vans became involved, they did it in a big way.

The tactic that the brothers utilized in building their financial empire was the holding company. In erecting the Terminal Complex, they established two companies to carry out the project; the Cleveland Union Terminals Company would build the station, and the Cleveland Terminals Building Company would develop the remaining properties in the group. As with their other ventures, where expansion was the keyword, the plans for the terminal also grew as time went on.

The Vans built well. Their retaining wall still supports Broadway Avenue (on the left). The rapid transit line is still operating. Weeds, however, grow where once tracks for passenger trains approached the Union Terminal.

themselves and their two sisters, Edith and Carrie, on South Park Boulevard. As their fortunes increased, they purchased a country estate in Hunting Valley which they named Daisy Hill. They spent some $3,000,000 there in building their country home, a 54-room mansion which they called Roundwood Manor. (The Daisy Hill property today is the setting for some of the area's most exclusive housing.)

Though the crash of the stock market in 1929 had weakened their control over their holdings, their spirit remained undaunted. Despite tightening credit, they purchased the Missouri Pacific a year later, a move that many observers felt was a critical error. The Depression grew deeper. Revenue from their many enterprises shrunk during the difficult times, but their obligations remained. In 1934 these amounted to $73,000,000, and the Vans could not come up with sufficient cash to meet them.

Growth continued to characterize the Vans' fortunes until 1929, a year that was to be fateful for millions across the country. Their vast business empire was spread across the country and was worth an estimated $4,000,000,000 at its peak.

The brothers' private lives also gave evidence of their wealth. Having never married, they had built a comfortable home for

A group named the Mid-America Corporation bought up their assets for about $3,100,000, certainly one of the great bargains in United States history. Mid-America was headed by two friends of the Vans, George A. Ball and George A. Tomlinson. These two, recognizing the business acumen of the brothers, brought them into the new corporation in a management role.

13

For a brief time it seemed that O. P. and M. J. had weathered the worst and were again on their way to the top. The severe pressures they had faced, however, proved to be more than just financial. M. J., the younger brother, was afflicted with high blood pressure. Weakened by the condition and exhausted by the events of the day, he was struck by an attack of influenza. It proved to be one challenge more than he could handle. He died in Lakeside Hospital on December 13, 1935.

O. P. survived his brother's passing, but the fire seemed to have gone out of his life. Always very close and dependent on one another, O. P. seemed to be lost without M. J. On November 23, 1936, aboard a private railway car, on his way to a business meeting in New York City, O. P. died during his sleep, having suffered a heart attack. He had survived his brother by less than a year.

As their empire deteriorated, so too did many other enterprises in Cleveland that had invested heavily in Van Sweringen projects. There were many businessmen in Cleveland who did not mourn the brothers' passing, reviling them for what they considered to be the questionable manner in which the Vans had built their pyramid.

Regardless of the judgments that history may make on their financial methods, there certainly can be no doubt about their positive contribution to the Greater Cleveland area. The Terminal Tower Complex stands today as a monument to them, and to their determination, vision and courage.

Cleveland erased its small town image and assumed the appearance of a major American city because of the dreams of two brothers who had faith in themselves and in their city's potential. Just as the Terminal stands today as the city's chief symbol, so too does it stand as the symbol of that spirit that made the city a great one.

From Shaker Square, the Vans routed their rapid transit tracks through Kingsbury Run and then on to the station on the Square. Here, just east of East 55th Street, the tracks of the Shaker and Windermere Rapid lines diverge.

CHAPTER 3

The Tower

Although work on site clearing and excavation had begun some three years earlier, the official groundbreaking for Cleveland's most famous landmark, the Terminal Tower, took place on September 28, 1923. General contractor for the project was the Cleveland firm of John Gill and Sons.

Architectural work on the Tower (and on most of the other buildings in the Terminal Complex) was done by Graham, Anderson, Probst & White, a nationally noted firm with main offices in Chicago, Illinois. Some students of architecture see in their design of the Terminal Tower some similarities to the New York City Municipal Building, designed by the firm's predecessor. For the firm of Graham, Anderson, Probst & White (they are still in business today), however, the Terminal complex in Cleveland represents their most famous achievement. The only other example of their work in the city is the 21-story Union Commerce Bank Building at East Ninth Street and Euclid Avenue.

When the Terminal development was first announced, the plan for the office building which would rise above the station called for a relatively squat structure. Rising some 14 stories, it was to be surmounted by a cupola-style central core of about five additional floors in height. Before construction actually began, however, the plan was changed. Management recognized how attractive office space in the new location would be. The cupola was replaced by a central tower that would rise another 38 floors above the 14-story base.

The Tower development pioneered a significant new concept in construction, the use of "air rights." Air rights involves erecting one building above the property of another, in this case the Tower over the Station. In a way it can be said that the Terminal Tower has no basement. The missing basement level is part of the Union Terminal's concourse area.

The original scheme for the Union Station did not include the central tower. It clearly lacked the visual impact that the subsequent plan provided.   (WRHS)

15

land. Unlike New York City (the skyscraper capital of the world, where bedrock is fairly near the surface), Cleveland, on the shores of Lake Erie, has a great deal of clay resting above its bedrock level. Thus excavation and foundation work in Cleveland is a more complex and often more costly undertaking.

The final plan for the complex provided for the soaring central tower. At the time it was built, the Terminal Tower's 42 floors made it the second tallest building in the United States.

To get to bedrock, the excavators had to burrow through several layers of clay of different consistencies. In some places it was fairly hard and dry. In others it was somewhat damp and plastic-like in quality. It is this feature that people often refer to as the "quicksand" upon which the Tower was built.

With the foundation in place, steel erection began in September, 1926. It proceeded rapidly, with the last piece of steel being hoisted into place at the 52nd floor level on August 18, 1927.

The cornerstone was laid on March 16, 1927. The task of attaching the limestone outer skin to the steel skeleton proceeded right along with the steel work, though at a slower pace.

While the Terminal Tower may not have a basement, it certainly does have a foundation. That foundation was laid by the caisson method; pits were dug through the ground down to bedrock, then filled with concrete. Each pit was dug by hand, to a depth slightly over 200 feet where bedrock was finally reached. As dirt was excavated from the pits, it was shoveled into large buckets and hoisted by cable to the surface.

Lore contains many references to the difficulties of erecting tall buildings in Cleve-

Enormous amounts of material were consumed in building the Tower. Over 55,000 barrels of cement were needed, along with 17,800 tons of steel, 118,230 tons of granite, limestone and terra cotta, some ten miles of water pipe, and some 71 miles of wiring. At the time, the cost of materials and labor for putting up the Tower amounted to some $11,000,000. At today's rates, to duplicate the feat would cost over $90,000,000.

By October, 1927 steel work on the Terminal Tower had been completed and the work of attaching the outer skin was well underway. The Tower was the second component of the complex to be built (the hotel was the first). (CPL)

The Van Sweringen Brothers commissioned artist Louis Rosenberg to provide a series of etchings showing the progress on the Terminal Complex construction. This 1928 sketch from across the Cuyahoga River shows the Tower complete, and work underway on the Union Terminal (at the left). (SHM)

The Terminal Tower fronts onto the southwest quadrant of Public Square. It can basically be described as consisting of a central shaft that rises 52 stories above the ground, with two 14-story arms angling away from the center and embracing the outer perimeter of the Square. On the southern side of the Tower, two additional wings, also 14 stories tall, extend from the central shaft to the Prospect Avenue line.

It is the central core that really forms the popular visual image of the Tower. It rises evenly through the 28th floor, where there is a structural change. It is here that the outer facing changes from limestone to terra cotta.

The central core continues from the 29th through the 34th floor levels at the same size as below, 98 feet square, but four pillars, extending from the 31st to the 33rd floor, break the smooth lines that mark the lower stories.

After the 34th floor the Tower narrows, but retains it basic square shape. Starting at the 37th floor, the Tower takes on a cylindrical shape. Additional pillars grace the 41st through the 43rd floor levels. At the 44th floor, the building narrows once again, and as it moves towards its 52nd story peak, its shape becomes conical.

Officially the Tower is listed as being 708 feet high, a measurement taken from the concourse level of the Union Station. It rises 786 feet above Lake Erie, and is 916 feet between the peak and the bedrock foundation.

18

The upper stories of the Tower reveal a multitude of architectural details. In this view of the top 18 floors, one can see the turrets, the two sets of pillars, the microwave discs, and the antenna. The area above the first set of pillars has never been used for any commercial purpose.

Rising above the Tower is a 65-foot high flag pole (now used as a radio transmitting tower), so that to the very tip of the pole, the height reached is 773 feet. Flag poles, however, are not counted as being part of the basic structure of a building; hence the 708 feet to the base of the pole constitutes the Terminal Tower's officially accepted height.

When the Terminal Tower was erected, it was the second tallest building in the United States, tallest in the country outside New York City (that city's Woolworth Building, at 792 feet, was the tallest). As the years rolled by, more skyscrapers were built in New York City that surpassed the Tower's height. The Tower maintained its position as the tallest in the country outside New

York City until November 6, 1967; construction on Chicago's John Hancock Building that day reached 722 feet. (That building eventually topped out at 1,127 feet.)

Demand for office space in subsequent years has prompted a proliferation of tall towers throughout the country. As a result of all this construction, Cleveland's venerable Tower is now ranked as the 35th tallest building in the United States and the 20th tallest outside New York City. Ten other United States cities now have buildings which exceed the Terminal Tower in height. The tallest building in the country at the present time is the Sears Tower in Chicago. It is 1,454 feet high and numbers 110 stories.

The view of the Tower from the south reveals arms extending from the central shaft. In this 1979 photo, one can see the progress that had been made in the cleaning of the building's exterior.

Cleveland's downtown has also experienced a building boom in recent years, with a dozen major office structures being added to the city's skyline. Despite the additions, the Terminal Tower has remained the city's tallest building. Certainly the economics of construction in Cleveland have helped the Tower to continue its reign as the tallest, but perhaps also a factor is the respect that it claims as the city's symbol.

The design of the Tower also plays a part in giving the building a soaring image that few of the nation's more recent skyscrapers possess. With its setbacks and the change of shape in its upper stories, the Terminal Tower seems even taller than it actually is. Contemporary buildings, in the interest of keeping costs down, tend to be boxlike in design. Although many taller structures have been built around the country, few of them have the visual impact that Cleveland's landmark continues to possess.

The main entranceway to the Terminal buildings is probably the most-used pedestrian accessway in the city. The upper reaches of the lofty gateway have been a perennially popular place with the pigeon corps as well.

The main entranceway to the Tower fronts on Public Square. It is an impressive one, featuring seven large arches, flanked by Ionic styled columns. Each of the arches, measuring 18 feet across and 35 feet high, contains a set of doors to the building. Above each door is an expanse of glass, filling the entire archway. The five center archways lead directly into the portico, while the outer two lead to the ramps that enter the traction concourses in the Union Station.

Through the arches, one enters the portico. At each end of the 153-foot long hall, there are entrances leading to the adjoining Stouffer's Inn on the Square and The Higbee Company department store. Rising into the portico are two ramps which connect with the Union Terminal's main concourse area. Directly through the portico one enters the elevator lobbies for the Tower, and an arcade which connects with

Prospect Avenue to the south.

The portico is an impressive room. It conveys a sense of spaciousness and elegance. Its floor is of Tennessee marble and its walls of Botticino marble. The northern wall consists largely of the five archway windows. The ceiling, some 47 feet high, features a vaulted configuration. It is made of precast ornamental plaster.

Seven murals grace the upper portions of the portico, the work of artist Jules Guerin. Set off by a cream-painted border, the murals depict commerce, industry, transportation, and the four elements: water, fire, air, and earth. The east and west ends of the portico have been enhanced in recent years by the addition of huge mirror panels which increase one's sense of the area's size. Greenery, too, has been added, providing the lobby with additional atmosphere. Hanging from the ceiling are five bronze-toned chandeliers.

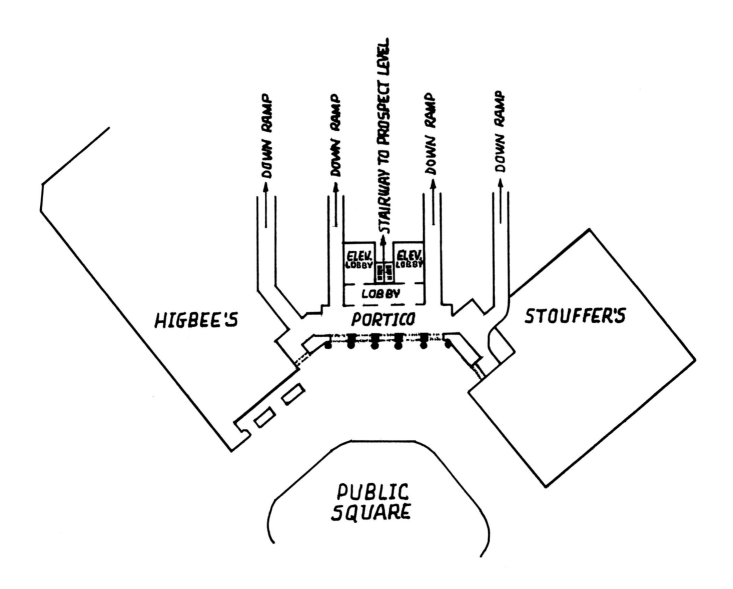

The portico, in a way, can be perceived as the unofficial grand entranceway to the city. Visitors who view it for the first time cannot help being favorably impressed by the combination of the room's brightness, size, and elegance.

Technically, the portico is not part of the Terminal Tower, but rather belongs to the Union Station below. The Tower's property line begins just through the portico. Maintenance of the portico, however, is taken care of by the Tower's management; in a sense, then, it can be said to belong as much to the Tower as it does to the Station.

Passing through the portico, one enters a smaller lobby. This connects to a stairway that ascends to the Prospect Avenue level of the building. At the top of the stairway an arcade runs to the Prospect Avenue entrance. To either side of the stairway is an elevator lobby.

Elevator service for the building is zoned, different banks of elevators servicing different levels. Altogether, counting the freight lifts (which are located elsewhere), there are 27 elevators. Elevator speed is 800 feet per minute. One can ride these elevators only up to the 32nd floor, however. Upward from that point to the 42nd floor, another set of elevators must be used.

From the 42nd floor to the top of the Tower there is no elevator service. From the 42nd floor to the 44th floor one can climb by means of a standard staircase. Then, from the 44th to the 51st, the only means of ascent is by a very narrow spiraling metal stairway that runs through the center of each level. The final floor is reached only by means of a small metal ladder.

The Portico has been renovated in recent years. Mirror panels at each end of the chamber reflect the light pouring in from the huge windows and from the string of overhead brass chandeliers.   (JM)

The Terminal Tower is probably the most photographed building in the city of Cleveland. As the city builds, new views of the landmark are always possible. Here it is framed by the new sculpture standing at the entrance of the Lausche State Office Building.

served any practical commercial purpose.

Tenant space in the Tower is confined largely to the fourth through the 43rd floors. There is some commercial space on the first floor (occupied by banking offices), and on the Prospect Level there are a few product and service oriented businesses. Office space occupies the fourth through the 41st floors. The 42nd floor (formerly the observation deck) is now a conference room. The 43rd floor is used to house microwave relay equipment. Since the Tower lacks a basement, the third floor is devoted to housing the building's mechanical equipment.

Over the years, the 42nd floor observation deck was one of the chief attractions of the Tower for the general public. When the deck opened in May of 1928, throngs of Clevelanders flocked to the site for a bird's eye view of

At first, this arrangement may seem to be somewhat strange — but in reality it is not. There was never any intention to use any floor above the 43rd (that floor served as a soda grill) for tenant space. In a way, the top nine floors exist only to give the building additional height for aesthetic purposes. The size of each of these upper stories is really too small ever to have

the city. In the 49 years that the observation floor was open to the public, there were seldom fewer than 50,000 annual visitors and often as many as 100,000. An examination of the guest book maintained on the observation deck reveals that the visitors were not just from the Greater Cleveland area, but from every state and from just about every country in the world.

The view from the observation deck of the Tower has always been pleasing to Clevelanders. To the southwest is the industrial heart of the city. The curving Cuyahoga River is in the foreground.   (JM)

To the north, the view from atop the Terminal Tower offers the open expanse of Lake Erie. The tall building to the left is the Justice Center, and to the right, the Anthony J. Celebrezze Federal Building.   (JM)

The developments of the Erieview Urban Renewal Project become apparent in this view from the Terminal Tower's 43rd floor. The tall dark building in the center is the Erieview Tower, the first major building to be erected in the Erieview area.   (JM)

Haze hangs over the city in this view looking east from the outdoor observation deck of the Terminal Tower. The Union Commerce Building, the only other example in Cleveland of the design work of Graham, Anderson, Probst & White, is at the center.   (JM)

Following their two-elevator ride to the deck, visitors were treated to a panoramic view of the city. On a clear day, from that height a person could see for a distance of 32 miles. Claims which some visitors registered, that they could see Canada from the deck, are not true; the Canadian shoreline is some 55 miles distant. Because of the curvature of the earth and the height of the 42nd floor, the 32 mile limit is the maximum distance one could see.

The observation floor was closed in April, 1977, and the space was converted into a meeting-conference room for the Chessie System, the building's chief tenant.

Just as the observation deck was one of Cleveland's best known attractions, the Tower also houses one of the city's best kept secrets: the fabled but little-known Greenbrier Suite.

While the Tower was under construction, the Van Sweringen brothers decided to have a suite of rooms built for themselves, so that on occasions when the press of business kept them downtown until late at night, they would not be required to travel back to their suburban home for a night's rest.

The suite that was designed for them can only be described as elegant. Built into an area of the Tower so that it actually intrudes on the space of Stouffer's Inn on the Square, the suite was equipped with a private elevator to make food service from the hotel's kitchen both quick and convenient.

The multi-level suite originally contained sleeping rooms, a dining facility and a spacious den with vaulted ceiling, balcony, and fireplace. Its rich paneling is of the Sherwood Forest design.

After the deaths of the brothers, the Greenbrier Suite was, fortunately, main-

tained. Today, it serves the Chessie System (the amalgamation of the Chesapeake and Ohio and the Baltimore and Ohio Railroads) as a private hospitality center. The sleeping rooms have been converted to additional dining space. The private elevator is no longer used. All food is prepared in the suite's own kitchen. But the authentic flavor of the original room has been retained, as has the elegance with which it was initially designed.

In 1975, the renowned interior decorator, Carlton Varney, was called in to refurbish the facility. Thus today, it sparkles with both antiques from the Van Sweringen era and a collection of other furnishings gathered from around the world.

Being a private facility, both in its original form and as it is today, the Greenbrier Suite is protected by an elaborate security system.

The portico, the observation deck, and the Greenbrier Suite are among the more interesting features of the Terminal Tower. The building, however, was built primarily as an office facility, and that remains its chief use to this day.

From the very beginning, Tower management has had no problem leasing space in Cleveland's most prestigious office building. The first tenant moved into the Tower in January, 1927, while construction work was still underway. It has been a story of successful leasing ever since.

Today the Tower has some 375 tenants, occupying about 610,000 square feet of space. Chief tenant is the Chessie System. Other tenants include law firms, realtors, investment offices, architects, and various types of business consultants. Altogether, nearly 3,100 people make the Terminal Tower their working home.

Keeping the building in good condition for its tenants and for the general public is the task of the Tower's owners and management. After the financial collapse of the Vans' empire, the Tower, operated by the Cleveland Terminal Building Company, went through a period of nearly 12 years during which the financial organization was completely reworked.

Between 1950 and 1964, the Tower's ownership changed hands five times. With the uncertainties that existed during the early years of reorganization and through the later years of frequent changes in ownership, there was some reluctance to provide the Tower with the full range of preventive maintenance services that might have been desirable.

All this began to change in 1964 when the Tower's current owner, U. S. Realty Investments (a Cleveland-based company), purchased the Tower for a price of $12,125,000. In 1968, U. S. Realty, through a subsidiary organization, also took over responsibility for the management of the Tower. In previous years it had been handled from New York City.

Along with local control of the Terminal Tower, local pride and vision returned to play their parts once again in the building's revitalization. Many improvements in the physical plant were undertaken. The old operator-controlled elevators were replaced by new automatic ones. Ceilings were lowered throughout the building. New air conditioning and electrical systems were installed. The portico was refurbished.

Improvements continue. Currently a ten-year plan is underway which will replace all of the Tower's 2,200 windows, at a cost of about $1,000,000. In the summer of 1979, a $650,000 exterior cleaning and tuckpointing program was begun. Because of the short season that Cleveland weather allows for such a job, four summers will be required to complete the project. When it is finished, the exterior of the Tower will be restored to the brightness that characterized it when it was newly built. Additional lighting, to better highlight the architectural details of the upper floors, is planned for 1980.

Clevelanders can rest content. Their grand old landmark remains in excellent shape 50 years after it was dedicated. It continues to fill the needs for modern office space. Because of its prestigious address and top-notch condition, it continues to operate as a high-demand facility.

The passing years, which have been good to the physical facility, have also contributed to the accumulation of a minor storehouse of Terminal Tower lore. It has been handed down by the generations that view the building as the main anchor of the city's identity.

Perhaps the most often repeated tale about the Tower deals with the construction workers who were buried beneath it. Versions of the story are numerous. Here are the actual facts.

In October, 1928, two construction workers were laboring in a pit which had been dug for the concrete foundations of the Prospect Avenue bridge structure. Patrick Cleary and Patrick Toolis were at the bottom of the pit, 103 feet deep, when they suddenly heard a roaring noise. The dirt wall of the pit in which they were working was giving way from the weight of the newly-poured concrete in the shaft adjacent to it! The men had no chance at all. Fifty tons of fast-hardening concrete engulfed them. It took rescue workers 18 hours to dig through the debris in order to recover their bodies.

Two more variations on a popular theme, the upper stories of the Terminal Tower take on some interesting details in these photographically-enhanced studies.   (JM)

Then, there is the story of the ghost of the Terminal Tower. Some years ago, as building inspectors were walking through an in-between-floors area, there loomed before them what appeared to be the body of a man. Recovering from their shock, they approached more closely to investigate. What they found was the legacy of a construction era prank. Apparently workers at the time had taken the coveralls from one of their colleagues, filled them with concrete, and stationed them in the dimness. The "ghost" still lurks in its original haunt.

The Tower and baseball in Cleveland were also associated. On days that the Cleveland Indians were playing at home, a banner was flown from the Tower's flagpole, just below the American flag. The baseball flag was discontinued many years ago, and the last U. S. flag flew in 1972. In that year a local radio station took over control of the flagpole for use as its transmitting tower.

Hoisting the flag above the Tower was no easy task. It took two men. First they had to climb ten flights to arrive at the portal at the base of the flagpole. There one man would exit onto a narrow metal grating and attach the flags to the ropes as the other worker handed them out to him. In the brisk winds that often buffeted the upper reaches of the building, it was not a task for the timid. Testimony to the severity of the winds is that in bad weather, a flag would last only ten days.

The other baseball connection with the Tower occurred in 1938 when it was featured in setting the world record for a high altitude catch. Two members of the Cleveland Indians baseball team, Henry Helf and Frank Pytlak, were stationed in Public Square to catch a baseball thrown from the very top of the Tower. The first few balls dropped attained a velocity of 202 feet per second. Hitting the pavement, they bounced upwards some 13 stories! Undaunted, the baseball players "hung in there" until each had made a catch, to the cheers of some 10,000 well-wishing onlookers who crowded the Square.

While other major construction has changed the Cleveland skyline, this photograph from the early 1970's reveals that the Terminal Tower continues its reign as the city's tallest and most distinguishable skyscraper.   (GCGA)

Sometimes it is asked if anyone ever jumped to his death from the Tower. One man did leap from a 42nd story observation room window. He landed on the ledge of the floor below. Dazed, but not seriously injured by his short fall, he was coaxed into the building by members of the Tower's security staff.

There have been other events that have marred the otherwise happy history of the Tower. In 1935 there was an apparent attempt made to blow up the building. A homemade bomb, containing six sticks of dynamite, was discovered by a tenant. The fuse had fizzled. Neither the perpetrator, nor his or her motive, was ever discovered.

Another unsolved mystery occurred when an axe was either dropped or hurled from the Tower's upper heights. The axe plummeted towards Public Square, crashing through the windshield of an automobile parked in front of the building's main entrance. There were three occupants in the car at the time. All of them miraculously escaped serious injury.

In recent years, the Tower again became the site of potential danger when in August, 1976, a veteran of the Vietnamese conflict held siege of the 36th floor executive offices of the Chessie System. He acted to protest what he viewed as the railroad's unrespon-siveness to hiring men who had fought in that war. After nine hours of holding his hostages, he was persuaded to release them and sur-render himself to the authorities.

The siege had unpleasant consequences for the Greater Cleveland community. It had revealed to officers of the Chessie System a flaw in the building's security arrangements. Visitors to the observation deck had to change elevators on the 32nd floor, in the middle of an area rented exclusively by the Chessie System. In order to tighten security and restrict those floors to employees, Chessie negotiated the closing of the observation deck, taking over that space for its own use. Despite pressure from the media and the public for the reopening of the observation floor, no satisfactory solution has yet been found to the problems that this would entail.

In the early years, the upper stories of the Tower had been brilliantly lighted by banks of lights on the 44th, 48th and 52nd levels. During World War II the practice was abandoned to conform with security requirements. The practice was not resumed until U. S. Realty Investments took over control of the Tower. Now once again, from dusk until midnight each night, the upper floors are bathed in bright lights — proclaiming, in a way, that all is again well with Cleveland's most famous landmark.

Standing alongside the Terminal Tower and looking up at its peak accentuates its sense of height. In this dramatic view, the Tower appears much taller than its stated 708 feet. (KK)

CHAPTER 4
The Union Station

A modern visitor to the Cleveland Union Terminal has a difficult time imagining the hectic atmosphere that pervaded the station in its early years. Today no more crowds throng through the Main Concourse. The sounds are gone too: the rumble of the arriving trains, the public address system announcing imminent departures on track such-and-such, the threads of conversations from people waiting for a train, the familiar call of "all aboard." All are gone.

The Union Terminal is, in a way, a memorial to a way of life that has largely passed from the scene. The railroad passenger train used to be king. Its throne has been usurped by the airplane and the automobile. Its stately palaces, the passenger stations, have been virtually abandoned, their splendor tarnished with the passing of time.

But let us look back to a happier time when trains were still THE way to travel, and when Clevelanders looked forward to a truly great union station.

Cleveland's union station was to be unique. Instead of a large and imposing edifice rising above the tracks, as was common in most major cities, Cleveland's station was built below ground level. The air rights above it were developed into major office and commercial space. With the exception of the clerestory for the Main Concourse, which stands south of Prospect Avenue between West Second and West Third Streets, there is no hint on surface level that a great railroad facility exists.

The Tower and the Hotel are already standing, but a vast hole in the ground marks the spot where the remainder of the Terminal Group structures will rise. Just about dead center, the Main Concourse of the Union Terminal will take form. (CPL)

33

Architects for this unique plan were Graham, Anderson, Probst & White. Chief engineer for the project was Henry D. Jouett. The New York firm of Aronberg, Fried & Company was the general contractor. Construction on the station proper began in May, 1928.

The original plans of the Van Sweringen brothers, to build a station for their rapid transit lines, had long since been revised. The station under construction was to be truly a "union" station, one which would house the facilities for all the passenger railroad lines serving Cleveland, and a terminal for rapid transit lines that would stretch out to all parts of the Greater Cleveland area.

The plans for the Union Terminal were so drawn that there was room for expansion to meet further growth needs by the railroads. But, from the very start, problems were confronted. The Pennsylvania Railroad, a major passenger service, decided not to use the new station, preferring to maintain one of its own. The capabilities for the station to be expanded were never exercised.

Work relating to the Union Terminal was not limited to the site of the station itself. Simultaneous with the activities at the downtown site, crews were also working on the east and west sides of the city, laying track which would merge in the new station on the Square.

In 1930, after years of planning and construction, Cleveland's new multi-million dollar Union Station stood ready to receive its first rail passengers. This view from the platform level shows the eastern approaches to the new facility. (SHM)

For many years Cleveland Union Terminal Company operated its own fleet of powerful electric locomotives to bring passenger trains from the downtown station to the city's outskirts. Here locomotive 221 is seen leading a New York Central train near West 25th Street. (RJC)

Steam was still the main source of motive power for the railroads when the Union Terminal was being built. The Van Sweringen brothers did not want the noise and dirt of a steam locomotive to pollute their new station, nor to disturb the tenants in the office towers above. As a result, they provided for transfer points to the east and west of town where trains would switch engines, dropping their steam locomotives for electrically powered ones.

The Union Terminal facilities are mostly below street level. The one exception is the clerestory (skylight) above the Main Concourse. The structure occupies the center of the parking lot located between Huron Road, Prospect Avenue, West Second and West Third Streets.

To accommodate the electrification plan, catenary and overhead wiring was put into place along 17 miles of track leading to the Union Terminal. The overhead system carried 3,000 volts of direct current. The Cleveland Electric Illuminating Company provided the power, which was then converted to direct current in the Union Terminal's own transformer station.

To bring the trains into the new facility, 22 powerful electric locomotives were purchased. These huge engines measured 80 feet in length, and were capable of up to 70 miles-per-hour operating speed.

Construction work proceeded at a brisk pace, and by 1930 the huge new station was ready to receive its first passengers. The facility boasted 734,000 square feet of space on its several levels.

The lowest level was called the track level. Altogether the terminal plan provided for a total of 34 sets of tracks, ten to be devoted to rapid transit use and 24 to serve the railroads. Demand never quite made all those tracks necessary. Eventually, only six tracks were laid for rapid transit use. Another 12 were put in for pasenger service, and one served as a running track. At the southern end of the facility, nine more tracks served as a coach yard.

Between each of the service tracks was a platform structure. These varied in length. The shortest of the platforms was 261 feet long, and designed for rapid transit use. The longest, 1,511 feet, was for passenger train service.

The platforms at track level were connected to the concourse level above by a series of stairways. Freight elevators provided for the movement of baggage, freight, and mail to the handling areas above.

Emerging from their trains, railroad passengers would climb one of six sets of stairways to enter the Union Terminal's main room, the Steam Concourse (also called the main concourse). This huge chamber measured 238 feet in length, was 120 feet wide, and had a ceiling 42½ feet high. In the center of the ceiling was a skylight (this is the area that emerges above street level in the block bounded by Huron Road, Prospect Avenue, and West Second and Third Streets). Complementing the daylight were eight huge bronze chandeliers.

The walls of the Steam Concourse were panelled in Botticino marble. The perimeter of the chamber was marked by 22 tall Doric Columns, 25 feet high, which added to the stately atmosphere of the room.

Entered through doorways that pierced the western wall of the Steam Concourse was a spacious waiting room. It measured 162 feet long, 56 feet wide, and 20½ feet high. It was built to accommodate 500 people.

On the eastern wall was the trainboard which listed the times for arriving and departing trains. Next to the trainboard was the entrance to a lunch room. Further south were a barber shop and lavatory facilities.

The southern wall of the Steam Concourse bears a huge mural. This artwork was not part of the original plan, but came in 1941 as a gift of the Cleveland Chamber of Commerce (predecessor of today's Greater Cleveland Growth Association).

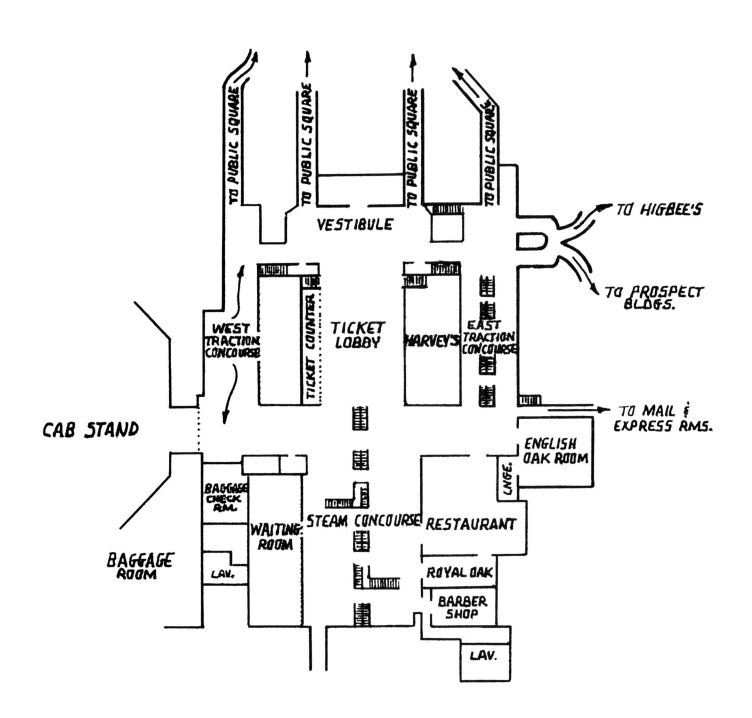

CLEVELAND UNION TERMINAL
CONCOURSE LEVEL

Today the Steam Concourse is an empty place. The floors and walls sparkle with the results of their recent cleaning; the ceiling, however, shows the neglect that is only now being remedied. The fluorescent lighting was installed in 1971 to provide illumination for the tennis courts, which were removed from the area during the summer of 1979.   (JM)

Executed in Cleveland by the Ferro Enamel Company, the mural was planned for the New York World's Fair of 1939. When the fair was over, the Chamber of Commerce felt that the mural should be brought back home. It was installed in its present location, together with a sign reading "Welcome to Cleveland." Not all of those who patronized the Union Terminal were in agreement as to the aesthetic value of the addition.

Adjoining the Steam Concourse at its northern end (towards Public Square), was a broad passageway running from east to west. It led to a taxi stand at its west end

and to the English Oak Room restaurant at the eastern end.

The cab stand was a real convenience to passengers. Alighting from their trains, they could wait indoors for a taxi that would take them to their Cleveland destination. Cabs arrived at the stand from West Sixth Street by way of a passage that led down to concourse level. This same passageway also connected to areas devoted to mail express, and baggage handling. The large area devoted to these services was located at the southern end of the terminal, in an area practically unknown to the general public.

Moving further north from the Steam Concourse, the central portion of the station (where the main entrance for the RTA Airport-Windermere rapid transit line is located today) was devoted to space for selling railroad tickets. Called the Ticket Lobby, this room was some 138 feet long and 92 feet wide.

Another passageway, running from east to west, adjoins the ticket lobby. Called the Vestibule, this passageway is pierced on its northern end by two ramps leading up to the portico and the Public Square level of the building.

The central portion of the Union Terminal complex is flanked on each side by two additional concourses named, respectively, the East and West Traction Concourses. Ramps lead from each of them directly to the Public Square level.

In the Van Sweringen scheme of things, rapid transit would some day serve the entire city. These two concourses were designed to handle the passengers from the suburbs who would be arriving and departing each day. The East Traction Concourse was designed with four sets of stairways to connect with the track levels below. Initially the West Concourse was not fully set up for rapid transit use. That development was not anticipated as occurring for some time.

The East Traction Concourse is the site for the entrance of the Shaker Rapid Division of today's Regional Transit Authority. The Shaker Rapid was the Vans' own line, and it was the only one ever to make use of the East Concourse. It first entered the Union Terminal in July, 1930.

Throughout the concourse level, the architects had planned room for a variety of concession space. Fred Harvey, Inc., a national firm servicing passenger facilities in various major United States cities, took out a lease for about 175,000 square feet of commercial space in the station. Newsstands, restaurants, gift shops, soda fountains, service facilities, all were under the aegis of the firm. Harvey's became a familiar name to Clevelanders who passed through the station. There were few who did not.

These facilities were designed to serve the needs of railroad passengers for years to come — a glittering, modern and spacious station in which Clevelanders could take pride.

The first regularly scheduled passenger train, a New York Central local from Norwalk, Ohio, pulled into the new station on May 19, 1930 to inaugurate a new era in Cleveland's railroad history. By that year, however, the railroad passenger business nationwide was already past its peak, and in a state of gradual decline! When the Union Terminal opened, some 80 trains were scheduled in and out of the city each day, although not all used the station. In the city's busiest year, there had been 94 intercity passenger runs.

Looking towards the Terminal buildings from East 34th Street, this scene from the mid 1960's gives a good indication of the extent of the central rail network. The set of tracks to the right, which continues beneath the series of bridges, carried both passenger trains and rapid transit vehicle to the Union Terminal. The large freight warehouse in the foreground is the site where the new main Post Office facility is being developed.   (GCGA)

By the end of the Second World War the number of trains had dropped to 49. Twenty years later, there were only 16 left; finally there was but one remaining, the Erie Lackawanna Railroad's commuter train which connected Cleveland to Youngstown, Ohio. It made its last run from the Treminal on January 17, 1977.

And then there were none. An era had come to an end.

Today Amtrak, a quasi-governmental agency, is responsible for running the nation's passenger trains. When it decided to restore train service to Cleveland with its Lake Shore Limited (with connections to Chicago, New York City, and Boston), Amtrak chose to avoid using the Union Terminal. Citing crippling costs of maintaining service in the giant facility for but one arrival and one departure each day, Amtrak found it would be considerably less expensive to build a new passenger station along the lakefront. Ironically, it stands today just a few hundred feet from where the old union station had been planned at the beginning of the century!

As the decline set in, the Cleveland Union Terminal Company, a subsidiary of the New York Central and Nickel Plate Railroads, sought ways to cut costs. With the advent of the diesel locomotive, the rationale of having electric engines bring trains into the Terminal was no longer valid. The expense of maintaining the overhead, the fleet of electric locomotives, the power stations, and the salaries for the extra crews involved in switching engines had all become prohibitively costly. It was decided to abandon the electric system, and the mighty engines ran in Cleveland for the last time in November, 1953.

Because of the high costs of operating the Union Terminal, the railroad owners were naturally reluctant to make improvements. For years, however, a public campaign had been waged to have escalators installed as replacements for the stairways to the trackside level. Finally, in 1952, bowing to the pressure, the railroads installed two escalators. These served only two platforms, and operated only upward. The railroads apparently felt that it was not as difficult to carry baggage down the stairways as it was to lug it up!

In 1955, some renewed traffic was generated for the Terminal as the Cleveland Transit System (predecessor of today's Regional Transit Authority) opened its new rapid transit line. The east side line opened for business on March 15, 1955, and followed the original right-of-way planned years earlier by the Van Sweringen brothers out to Windermere Station. The west side rapid transit began service on August 14 of that same year with trains travelling to West 117th Street. Subsequently the west side rapid line has been extended twice, first to West Park, then in 1968 to Cleveland Hopkins International Airport. This last extension made the City of Cleveland the first to have a direct rail link between its airport and downtown area.

A rapid transit car bound for the airport leaves the western edge of the Union Terminal property. The only tracks still remaining in the Terminal area are those of the rapid transit lines. Above is Huron Road and the new state office building.

But the decline continued. In 1970, the coach yards to the south of the station were covered over with asphalt. The resulting parking area could handle 1,200 automobiles. In a way the change seemed appropriate. It had been Americans' love for their cars which had led to the shrinking of the railroad passenger business. Stairways that once conveyed passengers to the train platforms below, now served in getting drivers to their cars.

What was in many peoples' opinion the greatest degradation of the fine old Steam Concourse took place in 1971. The marvelous chandeliers were removed, and fluorescent lighting installed. Alongside the stairways wire barriers were erected, and inside them two tennis courts were built!

In 1975, Harvey's closed its English Oak Room restaurant — for 45 years one of Cleveland's most popular dining spots. The lack of evening trade had made the restaurant a losing proposition.

While the decline of the station was going on, problems beset its owners. Bankruptcy overtook the Penn-Central Railroad which had become the deed holder for the Cleveland Union Terminal property. A declining facility was thus owned by a bankrupt company. There was no money available to provide for upkeep or improvements to the station. The decline accelerated.

At the end of 1977, Harvey's, Inc. reached the period when its lease of station facilities expired. The company chose not to renew, thus ending 47 years of Harvey's services in the Cleveland area.

Station watchers were thoroughly depressed at the deterioration which had beset the once spotless building. Paint was peeling from the ceilings. In places chunks of plaster had broken free due to water seepage from the street surfaces above. Security was lax, and gates had to be installed to prevent loiterers and vagrants from overrunning the complex.

There is a great deal of space on the Union Terminal's lowest level, mostly inaccessible to the public. Here a fleet of rapid transit cars awaits rush-hour service. The storage track area extends under Prospect Avenue to West Sixth Street.

At last, in 1976, a positive move was registered. The Penn Central Transportation Company had been formed to take over the properties of the former railroad. It entered into a new management agreement for the Cleveland Union Terminal property. The owners retained the successful real estate management firm of Ostendorf-Morris (a Cleveland company) to handle the station property.

Slowly but steadily, improvements have been made to the property. Security and maintenance have been beefed up. The ramps leading to the concourse level from Public Square have been refurbished. The tennis courts have been removed, and the Steam Concourse given a cleaning. The badly discolored marble walls have once again taken on a bright, clean appearance. The restaurant facilities (The English Oak Room, The Royal Oak, and The Acorn Room) have been reopened as a banquet facility. New tenants have been secured to occupy some of the space formerly used by the Harvey operation.

Today, there are 24 tenants in the Cleveland Union Terminal, with some 275 employees. Although the railroads have abandoned the facility (even the offices of Conrail — successor to the railroad business of the defunct Penn-Central Railroad — have been relocated) the Terminal is still a busy passenger place.

The Lausche State Office Building (left) has brought new vigor to the Terminal area. Its modern design and sleek lines offer an interesting contrast to the classic architecture of the neighboring Rockefeller Building. Superior Avenue is between the two buildings.   (JM)

Each day the Union Terminal serves as the chief station on the rapid transit lines of the Regional Transit Authority. Approximately 600 rapid transit trains enter or leave the station each day. It is estimated that approximately 45,000 pedestrians walk through the Terminal concourses each work day on their way to their place of employment or shopping.

Connected as it is with the Tower above, and with Higbee's, the Republic, Midland and Guildhall Buildings, the Post Office, and Stouffer's Inn on the Square, the Union Terminal's strategic location offers hope that it can look forward to a more prosperous future.

The most recent improvement to the complex comes from the construction of the new State of Ohio Lausche Office Building. It occupies the triangle of land formed by Huron Road, Superior Avenue, and West Sixth Street. Through a grant of federal government's Urban Mass Transit Authority, a tunnel will be built to connect the State Office Building with the West Traction Concourse — thus further extending the network of underground connections which makes of the Union Terminal a major pedestrian center.

There are many who expect that it is only a matter of time before the venerable old station takes out its second lease on life. An example of the station's continued attraction for investors was registered early in 1980. U. S. Realty Investments, owners of the Tower above, announced its interest in purchasing the station and transforming it into a smart shopping mall.

So, while the years have not treated the station as well as its towering sister overhead, no one is yet ready to count it out.

CHAPTER 5

The Hotel

The southwest corner of Public Square at Superior Avenue has been a popular location for hotel facilities. From almost the founding days of the city, the site has been occupied by buildings devoted to serving the weary and hungry traveler.

It was in 1815 that Phinney Mowrey, having invested $100 for a parcel of land at the corner of Public Square and Superior Avenue, began construction on a log structure that was to serve as a combination tavern and lodging house. Located across Superior Avenue from the city's first Court House, it was a popular place right from the start.

Five years later the land and lodge were purchased for $4,500, and Mowrey's Tavern was renamed the Cleveland House. Business continued to be brisk, and soon it became apparent that the existing structure could not meet the demand for space. In 1832 the old building was torn down, and a larger three-story facility was erected in its place.

In 1845 fire destroyed the Cleveland House. David Dunham bought the land and constructed a still larger, brick hotel which he named the Dunham House. Business continued to prosper, and an addition was joined to the four-story structure in 1850.

In 1852 the prospering hotel was enlarged once again and, under new management, was renamed the Forest City House. By this time the hotel was not only a popular resting place for the traveler, but was also a favorite gathering spot for Clevelanders. Its dining facilities hosted many a meeting of civic and political leaders.

The Forest City phase in the history of the property was both a long and distinguished one. It was the hotel where the presidents stayed and where many Cleveland organizations were born. The Forest City House lasted for 63 years.

As always when an era comes to an end, there was sadness in the city when the aging hotel closed its doors for the last time in September, 1915. As faithful as its service had been, the growth of the city required a larger and more modern facility to meet the increasing needs of a growing clientele.

* *

The Terminal Hotels Company (the name foreshadowed the future station development) purchased the land from its former owners, and the old structure was torn down. For an investment of $4,500,000, a thousand times more than was required to build the predecessor Cleveland House almost a century earlier, the new Hotel Cleveland rose on the site.

The architect for the new Hotel was Graham, Anderson, Probst & White. The general contractor was the Thompson-Starret Company. Rising 14 stories, the gleaming light grey building was faced with granite for the first three stories, and with terra cotta on the floors above. On its Superior Avenue frontage, the hotel was shaped like the letter "E"; on the interior there was a light well. This design was chosen so that every one of the 1,000 guest rooms could boast of a window and benefit from natural lighting. The windows, of course, were also of particular value during this era preceding the invention of air-conditioning.

Hotel Cleveland was the first element of the Terminal Complex to be built. Here it is seen shortly after its opening, before work had begun on clearing the site for the Terminal Tower.   (SC)

It was on December 16, 1918, to a city that was still celebrating the end of the First World War, that the new Hotel Cleveland was formally opened. A giant civic reception was held to commemorate the event, and the new building's dining facilities were given their first major test. The reaction of the throng was very positive. They were impressed by the tasteful decor and pleased by the good service.

The new hotel was an immediate success, one which was further increased when the Union Terminal opened for passenger business in 1930. Railroad travelers were pleased by the convenience that the hotel offered them. Alighting from their trains, they simply had to pass along the concourse level of the station, and up the ramps that led to the Public Square level. A turn to the left brought them right to the doors of the hotel, never having to face the uncertain prospects of Cleveland's weather.

The grand opening of Hotel Cleveland took place on December 16, 1918. Here a crowd celebrates opening night. The large number of flags and other patriotic gear was due to the city's continuing celebration of the Armistice ending World War I. (SC)

The Hotel Corporation of America operated the Hotel Cleveland through 1958, when the property was turned over to the Sheraton Hotel chain, and its name changed to the Sheraton Cleveland Hotel.

By the time that Sheraton had taken over management, the hotel was facing some problems. Railroad business had severely declined. Customers who had at one time been accustomed to the confined spaces of trains' passenger compartments, were now interested in hotel rooms that were more spacious and comfortable. The new owners also recognized that the hotel was lacking a dining-banquet hall of sufficient size to attract major gatherings.

With high hopes the Sheraton people poured money into the hotel. Rather than keeping 1,000 small rooms, the new owners decided to enlarge many of them and reduce their number. Extensive renovation led to conversion of the smaller units into 758

suites, and to rebuilding the top floor of the hotel into commercial office space.

The major involvement, however, was the construction of a new banquet hall and of a parking facility adjoining the hotel at its western end. The parking garage had become a major need, now that the principal mode of intercity travel had shifted away from the railroads. The banquet facility, the largest such facility between New York City and Chicago, was seen as a means of attracting much new business to the hotel. This addition provides the only example among the entire Terminal group of a structure in a different architectural medium. Despite this, the National Register of Historic Places says it "does not intrude excessively on the character of the whole group." After an expenditure of $5,200,000 the renovated and expanded Sheraton Cleveland Hotel looked forward in 1962 to a time of prosperity.

The year 1918 was exciting for the city. Just six days after Hotel Cleveland was opened, another major event occurred for Superior Avenue. Streetcars, like the one shown here passing the hotel, made their first plunge into the subway of the new Detroit-Superior High Level Bridge. (SC)

But despite the investment, only harder times were ahead for the hotel. Nearby, the new Hollenden House opened in the mid-sixties. It offered stiff competition to the Sheraton Cleveland. About the same time, many new hotel facilities were being opened near the Cleveland Hopkins International Airport, and along the interstate highways that brought visitors by car to the city.

As revenues began to decline, a series of complaints appeared in the news media about the hotel, alleging that its housekeeping was not up to par. In 1971 the Sheraton Cleveland management was told by the Cleveland Health Department to improve sanitary conditions on the premises.

The bad publicity led to a further decline in the fortunes of the hotel. In 1975 the Sheraton chain sold the hotel to the Cleveland Tower Hotel, Inc., a group headed by investor Thomas Lloyd. At the time of the sale, plans were announced for a major renovation of the facility.

But such was not to be. Affairs went from bad to worse for the hotel. and the property went into receivership in November, 1976. It was a tremendous blow to the city, another in a series of setbacks that seemed to give evidence that Cleveland was in a downward spiral. An attitude of helplessness seemed to prevail.

Sheraton management brought some major improvements to the aging hotel. The most significant of these was the addition of the ballroom-banquet facility and parking annex in 1962.   (GCGA)

It was at this point that an event took place which probably was more significant than simply the issue of the hotel's fate. Art Modell, president of the Cleveland Browns football team, and head of the Stadium Corporation, assembled a group of fellow Clevelanders who pledged themselves to take over the hotel and restore it to its former grandeur.

Modell's own Stadium Corporation had previously taken over the management of the Cleveland Municipal Stadium, after it had become a losing proposition for the city. His efforts led to a total renovation of the sports complex. Following the pattern set by that venture, Modell once again set out to rescue a failing enterprise. He brought together other prominent Cleveland individuals and corporations to deal with the Sheraton crisis. These included: F. J. O'Neill, the Stouffer Corporation, The Higbee Company, Eaton Corporation, TRW, Inc., the Chessie System, and the Diamond Shamrock Corporation.

Together this group commited some $18,000,000 to the purchase of the hotel property and for its renovation. The Stouffer Corporation became the operating partner in the group. At a sheriff's sale, the hotel was purchased for $4,000,000. On August 1, 1977 the hotel was closed, and the task of renovation began.

Under the direction of the Stouffer Corporation (no newcomer to the hotel business, the chain operates 21 hotels around the country), $14,000,000 was put into the restoration project. John Stauffer was named project manager, and a real transformation took place in the hotel as it neared its 60th birthday.

The group had determined that the renovation would not be a simple retouching of things, but a basic and complete renewal of the aging facility. Everything was to be redone, including the hotel's name. Hotel Cleveland, later the Sheraton Cleveland, was to be known in the future as Stouffer's Inn on the Square.

Stouffer management brought even more spectacular renewal to the hotel. The new marquee at the Superior Avenue main entrance shows the hotel's new name: Stouffer's Inn on the Square.   (SC)

The renewal of the building's exterior was the most apparent to the casual observer. The hotel's facade was steam cleaned and tuckpointed. The grime accumulated through 60 years gave way to a fresh clean light grey tone. The old windows throughout the facility were removed. New ones were installed, providing for greater energy efficiency and also adding a richer tone to the building's exterior.

The Superior Avenue entrance, with its grand stairway, had always been utilized as the building's main entrance. Traffic patterns over the years, however, made it more convenient for guests arriving by car to enter from the Public Square side. To change that pattern, a drive-up accessway was cut into the sidewalk on the Superior Avenue side of the hotel, and an attractive bronze-toned marquee was installed. The marquee, thoroughly skylighted, extends over the accessway, so that guests can escape the inconven-

ience of rain, sleet, and snow.

Up the grand staircase, the guest enters a totally redone lobby. This large room, totalling 9,200 square feet of space, had originally been ringed with shops. In their place is a continental style cafe, set off from the rest of the lobby by ferns and floral arrangements. Wall coverings are new, and the supporting columns in the room once again reveal their rich marble texture. Plush carpeting is underfoot and crystal chandeliers overhead. The lobby exudes an atmosphere of quiet elegance.

On the upper floors, the guest rooms have been totally redone. With an emphasis on space and comfort, the confines of those former 758 rooms have been eliminated, and 520 larger rooms built in their place. Thirty-eight are two-room suites, featuring luxurious appointments. All of the rooms have fresh carpeting, wall coverings, furniture, and new lavatory facilities.

Part of the renovation undertaken by Stouffer management included a complete redesign of the hotel's main lobby. Space formerly used for various commercial purposes is now reserved for guest comfort. (SC)

The meeting rooms, too, have been redone. Numbering 24 in all, they can accommodate groups as few in number as 20 or as large as 3,500. The most prominent of these is the Grand Ballroom. It has been extensively refurbished, with new carpeting and wall coverings. It can hold 2,500 people for a banquet, or seat 3,500 in theatre-style chairs for a meeting.

Commercial space in the Inn on the Square has been kept at a minimum. Besides a gift shop on the Superior Avenue level, only the space formerly occupied by the Kon Tiki and Minute Chef restaurants has been leased to commercial firms. The top floor of the hotel remains an office facility.

Perhaps the most widely acclaimed and most spectacular feature of the renovated hotel is the Atrium, now occupying the space formerly used as a light well for those rooms that did not face out onto the streets below.

What had been the proud claim of the old Hotel Cleveland management, that every room had a window view, was, in fact, less meaningful than it sounded. A large number of the guest rooms faced on-

to the interior light well. The only view this offered was that of another set of windows across the way. As the years passed by, the light well became rather dingy, the windows less than crystal clear, and the floor of the light well somewhat debris covered.

That once unattractive space today sports a very attractive lounge setting. The bottom level of the Atrium is on the fifth floor. It extends upward to the tenth floor. Overhead is a skylight. All along the five-story high walls are reflecting panels which accentuate the dimensions of the area. Guests who now look down from their rooms onto the Atrium see a brightly lighted area, with a swimming pool and bar. There is plenty of room to stroll and to relax. Rooms on the fifth floor have small patios which abut the Atrium's main floor panels.

The Inn on the Square features three restaurant facilities. On the lobby level, in the space where the old Falstaff Room was once located, is the new French Connection. On the Superior Avenue level there are two other restaurants, Mowrey's (named after the first inn on the site) and the Brasserie.

A major new feature of the Inn on the Square is a spacious atrium. Here construction is shown underway for converting an old light well into the attractive new lounge area. Renovation work was completed in 1979. (SC)

Although the entire renovation project had not yet been completed, Stouffer's Inn on the Square was opened to the public on September 22, 1978. As had been the case when the old Hotel Cleveland first opened in 1918, the re-opening was the cause for a celebration. Some 2,000 guests were at the inaugural festivities as a grand facility was restored to the service of the community.

Business for the hotel has steadily improved since the time of its re-opening. Besides being able to market the hotel's guest facilities and services, Stouffer's management can make the same claim on the intercity traveler that the old Hotel Cleveland once made: travel from home to hotel without having to face the elements.

The Inn on the Square can make that claim today thanks to the RTA rapid transit line which connects the Union Terminal with Cleveland Hopkins International Airport. Persons deplaning can enter the rapid transit station without leaving the airport building. The rapid ride downtown takes about 20 minutes, and the traveler is left just a ramp's walk away from the portico entrance to the hotel.

Another feature that is making the hotel better known to the community is the invitation to Clevelanders to enjoy a weekend at the hotel. Calling its invitation "L'Esprit Weekend", the Inn on the Square offers two differently priced weekend packages which include the overnight stay, dinner at the French Connection, champagne, breakfast in bed, and, of course, the amenities of the Atrium facilities.

The hotel on Public Square has made a comeback, and for that Clevelanders can be grateful. Once again a truly first class facility awaits out-of-town visitors at the city's center. But, as suggested earlier, there is greater significance to the restoration than simply the adding of one more hotel to the list of the other fine downtown guest establishments.

Over the years, Clevelanders have become all too accustomed to hearing about defeats for the city, or to hearing plans announced that herald new and exciting ventures for the downtown area — but with few of them actually ever going much beyond the publicity stage.

Of those developments which have taken place in recent years the majority have either been government funded or spurred by the kinds of incentives that federal programs have made less costly for the sponsors.

Yet in the case of the transformation of the Hotel Cleveland into Stouffer's Inn on the Square, a different spirit was evident, a spirit that has seemed to be missing from the city ever since the days of the Van Sweringen brothers. Once again civic pride united major figures within the Cleveland business community. They undertook a project, which, on the evidence of recent history, involved significant risk. They tack-

led the job, nonetheless, and they did not skimp on the dollars they spent. What resulted from their commitment is a facility in which Clevelanders take pride, and which brings an added share of excitement to the downtown scene.

Art Modell, the key figure in the renovation project, probably said it best on the occasion of the opening celebration of the Inn on the Square. He commented that the

> restoration of this fine old Cleveland landmark should help restore the lifeblood back into Cleveland's downtown. Like all major cities, we have had our problems in recent years, but with the help and investment of concerned leadership and by working together, which this project exemplifies, we can overcome them. Cleveland is a fine city and we strongly believe that our Inn on the Square, along with many other exciting new projects springing up downtown, can help restore Cleveland to its former greatness. And it can be done.

The new Stouffer's Inn on the Square stands as dramatic evidence that it really can be done. It also symbolizes the rebirth of a spirit that promises, once again, to poise the city for another giant leap forward.

The newly-cleaned exterior of Stouffer's Inn on the Square contrasts markedly with the darker walls on the Terminal Tower. In 1979, Tower management began a similar cleaning process, so both buildings will be restored to their original tones. (SC)

CHAPTER 6
The Prospect Buildings

If one were to mention the name "the Prospect Buildings" to most Greater Clevelanders, they would likely visualize either the famed rowhouses of the upper avenue, or perhaps some of the aging properties that line much of Prospect Avenue between East Ninth Street and Ontario Street.

Fewer would recognize that term as applying to the giant structure that fills the block bounded by Ontario Street, Huron Road, West Second Street, and Prospect

Three in number, the Prospect Buildings appear at first glance to be a single structure. The three buildings are joined together and share the same architectural style. A closer examination reveals that each has its own distinctive ornamental detail. Architect for the three buildings was, once again, the firm of Graham, Anderson, Probst & White.

In 1928 construction began on the first of the buildings, the Medical Arts Building (as

The Prospect Buildings form one of Cleveland's major office structures. See here from West Third Street, the Midland Building is in the foreground, and the Republic Building at the bend. The Guildhall Building's frontage is primarily along Huron Road.   (JM)

Avenue: an office complex housing some of Cleveland's best known corporations.

The relative unfamiliarity of the Prospect Buildings to the Cleveland public is due to their nature as office facilities. They have none of the attractions for the general public that mark their partners in the Terminal Complex. This does not diminish, however, the significant role that the buildings play in the economic life of the city.

it was then known). The second edifice was begun that same year, the Builders Exchange Building (also a former name). General Contractor for both of these was the Lundoff-Bicknell Company of Cleveland and Chicago. The third building, then named the Midland Bank Building, was started a year later. Its general contractor was the Aronberg-Fried Company of New York and Cleveland.

(Above) Construction work is well underway on Prospect Avenue and the Union Terminal, and just beginning on the Prospect Buildings. (SHM)

(Below) A year and a half later, April, 1930, the finishing touches are being put on the Midland Building. In the foreground is the site for the Post Office Building. (SHM)

The streets bordering three sides of the complex (Prospect Avenue, West Second Street, and Huron Road), are all actually bridges which straddle the property of the Union Terminal underneath them. The buildings themselves are also part of the air rights development. Like the Terminal Tower, they are built above land owned by the Cleveland Union Terminal Company.

Besides being joined together, the three buildings are also connected by an underground passageway to the East Traction Concourse of the Union Terminal. Thus, people can move to or from the buildings in shelter, and walk to the Inn on the Square, The Higbee Company, or Public Square.

The structures are designed in uniform 18-story height. In a setback design above the 18th floor are additional floors which hold the mechanical equipment. Like the Tower, these buildings have no basement. Faced with limestone, each building is ornamented in an art deco style. The massiveness of the structure is minimized by five eight-story recesses. The three on Huron Road and two on West Second Street also serve as light courts. There is also a light court extending the full eighteen stories on the Ontario Street frontage. The Prospect Avenue facade is solid, but because it follows the angle of the street, it gives a longer visual image to that frontage.

The architects' insight into the growing importance of the automobile is evidenced by their having included indoor garage space in the structure. Entered from Huron Road, the garage proved to be a popular feature of the group. Not only did this facility serve the needs of building tenants, but it also was an attractive parking area for downtown shoppers since they could reach The Higbee Company or Public Square by means of the underground passageways.

As office space needs grew, however, garage space was gradually reduced. Between 1953 and 1970 the garage, originally nine floors, was trimmed back to encompass but five floors. As the space was reduced, the convenience of the garage was reserved for the exclusive use of the lease-holders. The public was not unduly inconvenienced, however, as it was just about this time that the parking area immediately across from the Prospect Buildings (the former coach yards) was paved and converted to public parking use.

Other things have changed in the buildings as well. As its name indicated, the Medical Arts Building was conceived as a prime location for doctors' offices. In 1936, however, a new major tenant was taken into the building. Youngstown, Ohio's Republic Steel Company moved its corporate headquarters to Cleveland and settled into the Medical Arts Building. In acknowledgment of the new image the building was displaying, its name was changed in that same year to reflect the fresh situation, and the facility became known as the Republic Building.

As Republic Steel's need for space increased, authorities decided it should be met by not renewing expiring medical office leases. By the mid-sixties, the last of the doctors' offices had been vacated and the space converted for the use of the prime tenant.

The adjoining edifices have also undergone tenant changes over the years. The second of the structures to be erected, the Builders Exchange Building, was intended as a home for the construction industry. Its most prominent tenant was the Cleveland Builders Exchange; hence the name.

The Huron Road frontage for the Prospect Buildings offers an impressive view of the structure. Light wells were a valued feature of buildings erected prior to the advent of air conditioning. They also serve to break the otherwise massive appearance of the structure.

A feature of the building, quite popular with the general public, was the use of the 18th floor as an exhibit hall to spotlight developments in the building industry. Among the displays was a model home, dubbed the "home in the sky" because of its lofty setting. The display was a popular attraction for several years. When the Builders Exchange moved its offices out in 1941, the name of the structure was changed to the Guildhall Building.

The third building was designed to accommodate the headquarters of one of Cleveland's newer financial institutions, the Midland Bank. A famous feature of the new building was the expansive and elegantly-panelled main banking lobby. The Midland Bank's life was a short one, eventually being merged into the old Cleveland Trust Company (now AmeriTrust). As a result of the merger, a major banking facility be-

came available. In 1949, Central National Bank of Cleveland moved into the space; its previous headquarters building was torn down to make way for F. W. Woolworth Company's current downtown store. Central National Bank remained in the Midland Building until 1970, when it moved to its new tower at the corner of Superior Avenue and East Ninth Street.

A reminder of Central National's stay in the Midland Building remains; a huge sign bearing the bank's name is attched to the 19th floor setback of the building. Facing towards the west, the sign is visible from the other side of the Cuyahoga Valley. The famed banking lobby was no longer needed after the move, and although Central National Bank has kept a branch office in the Midland Building, it occupies only a portion of the former banking lobby area. The rest of that space has been put to other uses.

The lobby of the old Midland Bank was one of the most elegant in the city. The richly-panelled room was converted to other uses when Central National Bank moved to its new headquarters building in the early 1970's.   (CPL)

An interesting aspect of these three buildings, which combine to provide over 900,000 square feet of space, is that they house but four tenants. Three of these four represent some of Cleveland's largest and most successful industrial corporations.

The Standard Oil Company of Ohio (Sohio) is Cleveland's largest industrial company. It calls the Midland Building its headquarters, although its space is spread throughout the Prospect Buildings complex. In 1978, Sohio had sales exceeding $5,000,000,000. earning it 43rd place on **Fortune** Magazine's annual top 500 list.

The Prospect Buildings and the Tower are seen here from the western bank of the Cuyahoga River. In front of the building is a ramp which leads to the parking facility in the former coach yards.

Republic Steel Corporation, America's seventh largest metals manufacturer, is Cleveland's third largest industrial firm. It holds **Fortune** Magazine's 82nd spot on the basis of 1978 sales of approximately $3,500,000,000.

Sherwin-Williams Company is the third tenant in the complex. A major force in the United States chemicals industry, it is primarily associated with its lines of paints and coatings products. In 1978 Sherwin-Williams stood as the city's seventh largest firm, and was ranked nationally as the 239th largest industrial company, on the basis of over $1,100,000,000 in sales volume.

The fourth tenant of the complex is the Erie-Lackawanna Railroad. The operating aspects of the railroad have been merged into Conrail. The local Erie-Lackawanna offices house the trustees for the original road's assets and interests.

So, although the Prospect Buildings may not boast a high visibility factor with the general public, they represent some high-powered financial clout. From this downtown site, Republic Steel, Sohio, and Sherwin-Williams management overlook an industrial empire that employs over 80,000 persons. With operating divisions throughout the United States, Canada, and South America, its net income exceeded the $566,000,000 mark for the 1978 sales year alone.

60

Perhaps the least flattering view of the Prospect Buildings is from Broadway Avenue and Huron Road. Here the brick surface of the office structure can be seen. Originally, it had been planned that another building would be added at this point; hence, there was no reason to add the limestone facing.

There are several factors that have enabled the Prospect Buildings to continue to house these major tenants for so many years. Naturally, the central location and excellent public transit facilities have played a major role. So, too, has the convenient parking arrangement. But a more significant reason is found in the structure's unique management setup.

When the Van Sweringen enterprises collapsed in 1935, the buildings were purchased by an ownership group known as the Prospect Terminal Building Company. Later, ownership was transferred to an out-of-state pension plan. At that time the current management structure was set up. The four major tenants of the complex got together to form a management firm, which they named Ress Realty. (Ress is a mnemonic: "R" for Republic, "E" for Erie, and a twinned "S" for Sohio and Sherwin-Williams.)

The property was then leased by the out-of-state owners to Ress Realty, on terms that are renewable through the year 2010. Since the tenants are in fact also the management, it is clear that building maintenance and improvements are handled in such a way that the facility is of maximum service to the occupants.

It is also evident in the exceptional maintenance that has been provided throughout the three buildings. Maintenance work is done on a continuing basis, so as to avoid the necessity of facing unexpected and major repair needs. In 1979, a new roof was put on the buildings.

Another example of how well the self-operated management scheme works can be seen from the way Republic Steel Corporation's need for additional conference room space was met. To acquire the space, construction took place on the roof of the building, rather than on the inside. The result was the eye-catching stainless steel and glass structure that was built on the roof's southern exposure.

The Prospect Buildings are additional evidence of the solid foresight which the Van Sweringen brothers exhibited in the plans for the Terminal Group. For 50 years the edifices have stood the market's test: full occupancy and excellent physical condition.

The old coach yards were converted into a parking lot in 1971. The striped effect of the parking lot surfaces indicates where the tracks were once located. Huron Road is at the right.

CHAPTER 7

The Department Store

On the day that the Terminal Tower was formally dedicated, June 28, 1930, there was still a yawning hole in the ground where The Higbee Company's new downtown store was to stand.

The department store building, when it was completed a little more than a year later, represented the newest major retail facility in the city. It was also the newest home of Cleveland's oldest major department store company.

It was September, 1860 when the firm of Hower and Higbee opened its store for business on Superior Avenue, just west of Public Square. In 1902, following the death of co-founder John Hower, his surviving partner, Edward Higbee, had the store's name shortened to The Higbee Company.

The business was a thriving one, soon needing more space for merchandising. Higbee's built a new and much larger building at Euclid Avenue and East 13th Street to meet the growing customer lines. It moved into these new headquarters in 1910, the store's 50th anniversary.

Business continued to prosper. The lure of Public Square and the attractions of the newly-rising Terminal Complex, combined with the need for another increase in space, prompted The Higbee Company, under the leadership of its then president, Asa Shiverick, to commit itself to the new department store facility that was planned as part of the Terminal development.

In the early days of the century, the site of today's Higbee Company Public Square store was a collection of aging buildings. Humphrey's popcorn and candy store was located at the corner of Ontario Street and Public Square. The Humphrey family later moved on to the success of Euclid Beach Park.   (CPL)

Before its move to the new Public Square location, The Higbee Company was at the corner of East 13th Street and Euclid Avenue. That building later became the home of the Sterling Lindner Department Store, and today houses banking offices. (HC)

The firm of Graham, Anderson, Probst & White was called upon once again as designer. The proposed department store was to be the largest built in the United States over the previous two decades. At a cost of $10,000,000, the huge new facility was intended to be the epitome of modern retail merchandising concepts in an atmosphere that resembled more the private club than the public market.

Built adjoining the Terminal Tower, and bounded by Ontario Street on the east, Prospect Avenue on the south, and Public Square on the north, the Higbee store's exterior design and materials blend well with the other buildings in the complex. Architecturally, it acts as a balance to the hotel building which flanks the Tower to the west.

Besides easy access on three streets, the store also benefits from its connection with the other Terminal buildings. One entrance opens from the portico of the Tower; there

is also a basement store entrance that can be reached directly from the Union Terminal's concourse level. The basement entrance is at the end of the passageway that connects with the Prospect Buildings to the south, making shopping at Higbee's very convenient for workers in those buildings as well. The store rises 13 stories. Altogether, it contains over 1,000,000 square feet of floor space.

During the planning stage, the added floor space had been an important consideration for The Higbee Company. For the first time in its history, the store would truly be a complete department store. The new building allowed for departments that had not existed in the previous store. Added were housewares, furniture, glassware, carpeting, and sporting goods departments. Rich panelling was installed throughout the store to give it an atmosphere of quality and class.

The public anxiously awaited the new store's opening. Full page advertisements in the city's newspapers had kept them abreast of the building's progress. The advertisements proclaimed that the store would be filled with $5,000,000 of new merchandise. Almost nothing, either equipment or merchandise, was brought over from the old Euclid Avenue store.

Finally the building was ready. The lines were already quite long by the time the store opened its doors on Tuesday morning, September 8, 1931. Customers continued to pour into the store, more than exceeding the management's wildest expectations. By the time the store closed that evening, checkers at the doors had tallied a staggering total of 359,079 first-day patrons. The latest stage in the department store's history had been launched in a truly auspicious manner. It remains a success story to this day.

The hallmarks of the entire Terminal group's design were wise planning of space and solid construction. These have stood well the test of time. Little in the way of major reconstruction has been required to keep the store in tune with the changing needs of the shopping public.

The store today devotes nine floors to merchandising space, the basement through the eighth floor. The ninth and twelfth floors are devoted to office space. The eleventh floor is set aside for stock. The tenth floor houses the well-known Higbee Auditorium. Able to handle some 550 patrons, the Auditorium is a popular site for public meetings and a variety of social and cultural events. The tenth floor is also the setting for two of the store's four restaurants (the other two being located on the second and eighth floors). The thirteenth floor is used as housing for the building's water tanks.

In March of 1931, The Higbee Company's new home was rapidly nearing completion. The view is from Prospect Avenue. (HC)

Panelling was a key design feature of the new department store. Every effort was made to give the building a clublike atmosphere. The elevator lobbies are a good example of the concern for providing an attractive setting. (HC)

Only one major renovation was undertaken in the store. Sensitive to the needs of its shoppers, Higbee's recognized that the existing escalator and elevator system was inadequate for the comfortable movement of the store's patrons. In 1956 a second set of moving stairways was installed.

Flanking the elevator lobby to the opposite side of the older escalators, the new moving stairways were designed to move patrons at a speed of 120 feet per minute as compared to the 90 feet per minute of the older ones. Shortly after their installation, however, store officials noted that the increased speed of the descending escalators was proving somewhat too fast for the safety of the elderly customers. The speed was subsequently reduced, back to 90 feet per minute.

The location of the elevator lobby and escalator corridors has been widely praised as one of the store's most attractive design features for maximum patron convenience. They are located in the center of the store; yet they are arranged in such a way as not to intrude on the most effective use of floor space.

On the first floor, the elevator-escalator corridor is set off to one side, leaving the entire main sales area unobstructed. This feature is made possible by the main floor actually being comprised of two levels, the Ontario level and the Prospect level. On the upper floors, the space of the two levels is united in one, thus accounting for the central location of the elevator-escalator system above.

Different approaches to merchandising are apparent in these two views of Higbee's sales areas. Above, the austere appointments were characteristic of the old East 13th Street Store. (HC) Below, the first floor of the Public Square store is brightly lighted and the merchandise attractively displayed. (JM)

The Higbee Company auditorium on the tenth floor has long been a popular site for various kinds of community and civic meetings. It is also headquarters for Santa Claus during the Christmas shopping season. (HC)

For many years, to go shopping meant to go downtown. The Higbee Company, of course, was one of the chief shopping places in the central area. But the population exodus to the suburbs and the increasing use of the private automobile for shopping changed that pattern. Large outlying shopping strips (and later enclosed malls) took a toll on the downtown retail shopping trade.

The decade of the 1960's saw many changes in downtown retailing. Familiar downtown department stores were closed. The Bailey Company store at the corner of Prospect Avenue and Ontario Street (across from Higbee's) was torn down. Its site was used for a mammoth parking garage.

Taylor's Department Store was also closed; its building was converted into office space. Sterling-Lindner's also closed its doors. Part of its building was torn down and the rest of it (the earlier Higbee building) was renovated into space for banking purposes.

The Higbee Company was alert to the changes that were affecting the retail business. In 1961 the firm opened its first branch store in the Westgate Shopping Center, on the northwest side of town. Since then, Higbee's has opened six other suburban stores, as well as more distant stores in Elyria, Canton, and Youngstown, Ohio. The Higbee chain today numbers eleven stores in all.

The Higbee Company's ongoing efforts have kept the Public Square store an attractive one. Crystal chandeliers and a red carpet for the main aisle were added to give the first floor a brighter and richer tone. *(JM)*

between the hours of 8:00 a.m. and 6:00 p.m., downtown Cleveland has the greatest population density in the State of Ohio. With the more than 250,000 downtown workers as potential customers, the main store is a very convenient place for shopping during and just after the work day.

The second factor that accounts for the downtown store's continued sales leadership is the facility's size. With almost half (500,000 square feet) of its entire floor area devoted to selling space, the main store has a greater capacity than any suburban outlet for both the display and the selection of merchandise. These assets combine into a major attraction for the discriminating suburban shopper.

While major renovations of its downtown facility have not been called for, Higbee's has, nonetheless, continued

Despite the company's significant expansion into suburban shopping centers and the habits of many Greater Clevelanders who shop exclusively in the suburbs, Higbee's downtown store remains the chain's sales leader by a significant margin over the suburban outlets.

Two major factors probably account for the downtown store's continued success. The first centers around the fact that

to spend money to keep its Terminal group store attractive to patrons. Besides the installation of new escalators, remodeling has been done on the second through the fifth floors. This has made shopping more convenient and made for a more contemporary atmosphere. In 1979 Higbee's devoted its efforts to expanding the basement sales area and relocating some of its less substantial products (greeting cards and candy) away from the first floor sales area.

In 1980 The Higbee Company will celebrate its 120th anniversary in the retail business. The downtown store remains a keystone in the firm that now covers northern Ohio with eleven stores.

scene of bustling shoppers and the sights and sounds of the holiday season. Overhead, running the length of the store, were huge shiny bells, rocking back and forth. Christmas trees and Christmas colors were everywhere. Excitement built as the youngster moved towards the escalators (these, too, could be fun) and ascended to Santa Claus's headquarters.

The line of children waiting their turn for a chat with Santa was usually a long one, but it was worth the wait. Each child would have many requests to make for Christmas presents; the wondrous passage through the store undoubtedly had provided the imagination with a few additional items for the Christmas "want list."

Then it would be time to return home. But before heading out to the streetcar or bus stop, there would be one final trek to the basement for a "frosted malted," a drink served so delightfully thick that it seemed it would last forever.

These are the kinds of memories that surge from the soul of the Greater Clevelander who visits Higbee's downtown store during the Christmas holiday season. The silently tolling bells are now gone, but if anything, the store's sparkle has only increased (and one can still secure a frosted malted — though they are now served in throwaway cups).

Cleveland's once newest department store building is no longer very new, but it continues to exercise its sales leadership over its younger brothers and sisters in the chain. It remains for many, with its sustained atmosphere of quality merchandising, a perfect example of what a real department store is supposed to be.

For most Clevelanders, however, the importance of the Higbee Company's downtown store is not related to either its design features or its leadership in sales. Rather, the store's significance is related to the kind of impressions that it made on them when they first visited it as children. These impressions are now imbedded in fond memories, most vivid of which are those connected with the annual visit during the Christmas shopping season.

Entering the store through one of its revolving doors (which could be an adventure in itself), the youngster was confronted by a

CHAPTER 8

The Post Office

The last of the structures to be built in the Terminal Complex became the main headquarters of the Cleveland branch of the United States Post Office. The new building replaced the previous post office structure which had been located on the northeast corner of Superior Avenue and Public Square. The older building was converted to other governmental purposes and today serves as the Cleveland home for the federal courts.

an attractive one. The old Public Square main office had been positioned without due regard having been given to the importance of railroad access for the receipt and delivery of the mails. The new building, adjoining the Union Terminal, was considered to have an ideal location.

Architects for the Post Office building were different from the firm that had designed the rest of the Terminal Complex. As a government facility, the Post Office

Before it moved to the Terminal Complex, the United States Post Office was situated at the corner of Superior Avenue NE and Public Square. The building today serves as the Federal Court House.   (USPS)

In February, 1932, construction on the new main post office building was begun, using a foundation which had been put into place earlier as part of the overall Terminal Complex planning. Its site, occupying a total of 99,000 square feet, is bounded by Huron Road, Prospect Avenue, West Third and West Sixth Streets. As is true of the Prospect Buildings, its sister edifices to the east, the Post Office is flanked by roadways which are, in fact, bridge structures.

The site for the new postal facility was

was designed under the guiding hand of official United States Architect, James A. Wetmore. Local architects for the project were the Cleveland firms of Walker & Weeks and Philip L. Small. Since the Post Office was built as a government facility, at government expense, it was never directly under the control of the Van Sweringen enterprises. Like the rest of the group, however, it was built on air rights over the property of the Cleveland Union Terminal Company.

Construction on the new main Post Office Building began in 1932. The structure was placed on a foundation which had been built earlier as part of the overall planning for the Terminal development site. (USPS)

The cornerstone for the Post Office, laid on February 16, 1933, became the center of a mystery the very next day. It had disappeared overnight. The explanation to the mystery, however, turned out to be a simple one.

The cornerstone-laying ceremony had been rushed ahead of its natural schedule so the stone could bear the names of the Herbert Hoover administration in Washington, D.C., which was about to leave the White House. After the ceremony had been completed, construction workers had merely removed the stone so that it would not be damaged by the construction work still needed before it could be permanently set into place.

Two and one-half years after construction had begun, on September 3, 1934, the formal dedication of the new facility took place. The dedication ceremonies were the focal point of a public celebration (the community had little else to cheer about during these deep days of the Great Depression). The dedicatory plaque placed in the Prospect Avenue Lobby bears the names of members of the administration of Franklin D. Roosevelt, which had succeeded Hoover's to power. Thus the cornerstone and the dedication plaque give credit for sponsorship of the construction project to two different presidencies.

The Post Office Building is the only one of the Terminal Group to be completely surrounded by bridges. Here one can clearly see the bridge structure for Prospect Avenue. To the right is the ramp entrance to the lower-level driveways and the old taxi stand. (USPS)

The main lobby of the Post Office Building extends from Prospect Avenue to Huron Road. This early photograph shows the art deco motif that was employed in the building's furnishings. (USPS)

The main office of the Cleveland Post Office boasts a total of 494,000 square feet of space on its six levels. The lowest level is below the street surface, and can be entered by a roadway from West Sixth Street. This roadway also leads down to the concourse level of the Union Terminal. Part of it branches off to reach the old taxi stand area. It also connects with an interior roadway located to the south of the Steam Concourse which extended to the old freight elevator bank that served the track level. It was in this area that mails were transferred to and from the trains.

From the exterior, one would judge that the building had four floors above ground level. There are, in fact, five floors. The top floor is windowless, and serves as the mechanical floor for the facility (once again, the building is without a basement).

The first through the fourth floors are devoted to processing the mails. The first floor, probably the one most familiar to Greater Clevelanders, houses the main postal services lobby.

Entered from either the Huron Road or the Prospect Avenue sides, the main lobby runs across the width of the building. The lobby's marble walls are pierced along both sides by service windows to accommodate the public. Above the windows is a series of marble reliefs, executed by artist Frank Jirouch, which depicts the history of progress in the mail delivery system in the United States. The center of the lobby is fitted with customer service tables allowing a place for postal patrons to complete their mailing tasks. There is also a philatelic boutique, offering postal items to stamp hobbyists.

A mural graces the main entranceway. Painted by Cleveland artist Jack J. Greitzer, the mural depicts the tasks of those in the building working to prepare the mails for delivery.

The remainder of the first floor is set aside for use as the processing center for mail in the downtown delivery zones. The second, third, and fourth floors are used for handling the mails for the rest of the Cleveland postal region. Administrative offices for the postal system are also located on these floors.

The main Post Office is a busy building. Its area of service is far larger than just the City of Cleveland and its suburbs. Outgoing mail is processed for a geographic area that stretches from Conneaut on the east to Vermilion, Ohio on the west, and south to the borders of Cuyahoga County. Incoming mail is handled for five sectional areas comprising postal zip code zones 439 through 447 (Cleveland and its many suburban branches are designated as zip code area 441).

The Post Office Building was designed to provide for a great deal of flexibility. That feature has proved to be a real asset, as the manner of working with the mails changed dramatically following the 1930's. From a largely hand-sorting process, technology has brought about a major transformation which now allows huge and complex machines to speed the mailing operation.

Yet with the volume of mail constantly increasing (today an average 1,000,000 pieces are handled each day by the main Post Office), and with the railroads no longer playing much of a role in the intercity delivery process, it became clear to the postal authorities that major changes were required. Even the addition in 1954 of the Parcel Post Annex on the lakefront did not significantly delay the need for facing the fact that the Main Post Office was no longer able to provide for future growth needs.

In the late 1960's it was decided that Cleveland needed a new main Post Office. Plans aimed towards a grand opening for the new center in 1971. A series of problems and delays set the date back another eleven years. It is now expected that the new facility will be ready for service in late 1982. The new center will be located in the area framed by Orange and Broadway Avenues, between East 14th and East 30th Streets. In 1979, the major portion of the site was cleared by razing several dilapidated warehouse buildings that had stood in the location for years. The new main Post Office will be built with only one level, better to handle the modern postal technology, and will once again combine parcel and regular mail handling under one roof.

Despite its plans for a new building, the United States Post Office (renamed the United States Postal Service in 1971 as part of the Postal Reorganization Act) did not hesitate to do its duty when, on January 2, 1976, a six-ton slab of stone facing fell from the building, crushing an unoccupied automobile parked below.

A careful examination revealed that other slabs were also loosened, probably due to the years of vibration caused by heavy vehicles passing over the bridges that surround the building. Safety dictated that repairs be made.

In mid-1979, the new exterior facing of the Post Office Building was almost completed. The renovation project cost over two million dollars.

Since the Post Office Building was part of the Historical Landmark designation that had been given to the entire Terminal Complex in 1976, the law stipulated that the original design features of the building be maintained. The Postal Service committed itself to a total resurfacing of the building. Beginning in 1976, the original facing was removed, and in its place new sections of pre-cast concrete were fitted. Those sections of the original facing which bore ornamental detail were removed, cleaned, and then hoisted back into position. The re-facing project, at a total cost of $2,030,000, was completed in 1979. The Post Office Building joined the Terminal Tower and Stouffer's Inn on the Square in sporting a bright new exterior.

The future use of the building has not as yet been determined. When the Post Office moves into its new facility, the old building will become surplus property. United States law dictates that surplus governmental property be first offered to the General Services Administration (GSA) for its use. In the unlikely event the property is not wanted by that agency, (there is need to consolidate federal offices now scattered about the city) it is, in turn, to be offered next to the State of Ohio, then to the county, city, and the school system. If none of the governmental entities is interested, the property can then be placed out on bids to any interested party.

So, while its future is not clear, it seems safe to assume that a newly-repaired facility, with a large amount of floor space, in a prime location, would present an attractive opportunity for some commercial venture.

Knowledgeable parties are convinced that the handsome rectangular building which has served so well the communications needs of the area will enter its second fifty years of existence with a renewed value to a robust downtown.

This is an architectural rendering of the new Main Post Office Building. Site clearing for the development began in 1979. Completion of the building is expected by the end of 1982.   (USPS)

CHAPTER 9
Possibilities and Problems

As part of the community's salute to the newly-completed Terminal project, the Cleveland **Plain Dealer** published a special section in its Sunday, June 29, 1930 edition devoted to the Union Terminal development. Echoing the sentiment that filled the community at the time of the dedication ceremonies, the paper stated that "It is no wild guess to predict that buildings will still be erected on property owned by the Van Sweringen Corporation twenty-five years hence."

Of course, time proved that prediction to fall far short of accuracy. It was not until 32 years later, in 1962, that any further construction took place on the site, that being the banquet hall addition to the hotel. The Great Depression had effectively blocked the carrying out of the other developments that had been planned.

And other plans there were. One of them involved completion of the block partially filled by the Prospect Buildings. For years a grey wooden fence stretched from the edge of the Republic Building on Ontario Street to the point where it meets Huron Road, and then along Huron to the edge of the Guildhall Garage. (In 1977 that unattractive fence was replaced by Ress Realty with a multi-colored metal one.)

A look over the top of the fence today reveals the abandoned track bed and the ends of the railroad passenger loading platforms below. One also glimpses the tracks still in use by the rapid transit trains serving the east side of the city. If one were to raise his eyes, he would notice that the wall of the Guildhall Building is covered with brick rather than limestone, and that the edge of the Republic Building also shows a mixture of brick along with the standard limestone facing.

This early sketch of the Terminal Complex reveals the extent of the plan for developing the downtown site. The financial troubles which brought down the Van Sweringen empire prevented the completion of the project. (SHM)

77

The brick was not meant to be a permanent outer facing. Plans had been made to erect another office tower within the perimeter that is today marked by the fencing. Its outlines would have covered the area where the brick is now visible, and its facing of limestone would have blended perfectly with the adjoining structures.

Another tower was to have risen in the block bounded by Prospect Avenue, Huron Road, West Second and West Third Streets, in the area today serving as a parking lot, and where the roof above the Union Terminal Steam Concourse skylight now stands. The foundations had been laid for a 20-story, 500,000 square foot building to fill in the gap which now exists between the Midland Building and the Post Office. The foundation remains today, but no building was ever begun.

The remaining site is in the triangle formed by Prospect Avenue and Superior Avenue, to the west of Stouffer's Inn on the Square. Architects' sketches reveal that the entire area was to have been filled by another tower which would have connected with the hotel building. Here the wooden fence still remains, protection for pedestrians from a fall to the rapid transit tracks below.

It was the demise of the Van Sweringen empire that halted these further developments and which made the **Plain Dealer** prediction go unfulfilled. By the time the existing structures had been completed, the effects of the Depression were such that no new building could reasonably be undertaken.

When the worst days of the Great Depression had passed and business was once again on the upswing, the kind of forward thrust that had been typical of the City of Cleveland over its first 134 years of existence had been replaced by a new spirit. The new tone was characterized by a cautious and conservative approach.

Not only was the remainder of the Terminal Complex never completed, but no other major office tower construction occurred anywhere in the city until the mid 1950's. Then the Cleveland Electric Illuminating Company put up its new headquarters building across from the Terminal Tower, on the northwest quadrant of Public Square. When major new development was finally undertaken, the thrust had moved eastward from Public Square to the area around East Ninth Street. It was in this area that Erieview, the urban renewal project so long promoted by The Cleveland **Press,** was translated from the planners' sketches to the sleek modern office towers that exist today.

The positive effects of the Erieview Project, together with the increasing demands for modern office space, have also prompted several proposals for further developments in the Terminal area.

The most exciting of these plans, named the Tower City proposal, was announced in 1972. Sponsored by U. S. Realty Investments (the firm which owns the Terminal Tower), architect for the development was the Cleveland firm of Dalton, Dalton, Little & Newport. Variously estimated at between $250,000,000 and $350,000,000 in cost, the plan envisioned developing the area to the south of Huron Road down to the Cuyahoga River. Among the features of the plan were a 1,000-room hotel, three office towers, a parking garage for 6,500 cars, a sports arena, an air cargo terminal, and several apartment buildings.

This 1929 view of the Terminal site reveals two areas where buildings were planned but never constructed. The triangle of land at the bottom of the photograph and the square of land adjacent to the Prospect Buildings remain empty today. (CPL)

Another slice of land that was not developed lies at the corner of Ontario Street and Huron Road. A glimpse over the protective fencing shows weeds growing where passenger trains once ran. (JM)

One of the reasons for the plan's failure to materialize is a major problem that continues to beset the Terminal Complex properties.

In the Ordinance of 1919, it was specified that the City of Cleveland would be the agent responsible for the upkeep of the surfaces, curbs, sidewalks, and the water lines of the streets that were being erected on bridgework in the Terminal Group area (Huron Road, Prospect Avenue, West Second, Third, and Sixth Streets). The ordinance further stipulated that the Cleveland Union Terminal Company would have responsibility for maintaining the underlying structural steel bridge work.

Over the years, the bridges in the project area have shown signs of considerable deterioration, as have bridges throughout the city. Because of the mutual responsibilities involved with the Terminal bridges, however, there has been a great deal of controversy as to which party is to pay for what portion of the needed repairs. The city, experiencing serious financial problems, has been reluctant to accept the amount of liability that the property owners feel is its rightful share.

Considerable damage has been done by water leaking through from the roadways' surfaces. Over the Union Terminal concourse level, there are eighteen defective expansion joints. The ceilings in the traction lobbies show severe damage to the plaster work. Repairs to the water lines have been of a temporary rather than a permanent nature.

Tower City's failure to materialize was due, at least in part, to the inability of the parties to settle the bridge repair problem. As time passes, with no repair work being undertaken, further deterioration and an escalating repair bill are the result.

In July, 1977 the firm of Cushman-Wakefield of New York City proposed a $70,000,000 office development on the location of the old coach yards. The plan would have provided for a 22-story office building, with an atrium connecting the office tower to a completely redesigned Union Terminal Main Concourse. All told, the plan would have provided 975,000 square feet of space with the Standard Oil Company of Ohio (Sohio) being the prime tenant. The City of Cleveland was to have contributed towards the repair of the bridges as its share of the project. Once again that proved a snag, and time for the project expired. It was declared dead in July, 1978.

There have been other plans for the area as well. At one time a giant hotel was proposed for the coach yard site, along with a series of exclusive shops. An airline ticketing agency has been proposed for the Terminal concourse, using the RTA Airport Rapid Transit line as the connecting link. The concourse has also been seen as an ideal site for an intermodal transit station, mixing busses and rapid transit service without requiring the passengers to climb to the square for a transfer.

The most encouraging event for the Terminal Complex area has undoubtedly been the erection of the Lausche State Office Building at West Sixth Street and Superior Avenue. The 13-story trapezoidal structure is headquarters for the Ohio Lottery as well as for the Regional Transit Authority. Its location does much to anchor that part of the entranceway to downtown, and its working population will be an additional incentive for further development in the area.

There are problems which remain to be worked out, but downtown real estate men insist that further enhancement of the Terminal area is a "logical development." As the Terminal Group celebrates its golden anniversary year, the signs are positive.

The Tower has been improved. The Station has new leadership. The Hotel has been transformed. The Prospect Buildings are thriving. The Department Store remains a sales leader. The Post Office beckons for new involvements. Civic leaders have shown that they can work together for a common cause. The political climate seems to have turned away from confrontation towards a spirit of cooperation.

Cleveland's great symbol stands proud as it enters it second half century. Yesterday's vision, today's reality, it also stands as a promise of an exciting tomorrow.